FROM MAD

THE OLIVE GROVE

REENGINEERING RETIREMENT

By V.F. Gutierrez

Dedication

To Grace, my mother-in-law, who is now more than ninety-five years old. For over twenty years, she has been my counselor, guide and friend. Her continuous nudging drove me to record and then write about our experiences.

Table of Contents

Prologue

On December 1, 2015, my wife, Susan, said to me, "Few would believe what has happened in the last fifteen months. My Tuscan dream is now a Mexican dream and it will take an entire book to relate what has transpired in the last fifteen months. So start a new book."

Today is Saturday, August 6, 2016. Last week, I sent my first book, *The Light of the Serene Moon*, to the printer, and I expect that soon it will also be available on Amazon.com. That book took me almost eight months to finalize due to the hectic activity of our evolving olive-oil venture.

Today is a special day: it has been exactly two years since we made our first olive oil; this great moment changed our lives, and therefore today is the perfect time to begin recounting these recent events. We hope you will enjoy the story that follows.

Learning about Olives: July 2014

Four days after retiring on June 30, 2014, to San Miguel de Allende, Guanajuato, Mexico, I realized that the anxiety of having very little to do was driving me crazy. Prior to this, I had resided at our home in Mexico for eighteen months, working nearly seventy hours per week for my employer and traveling to New York every eight weeks. I had believed and even bragged that I had transitioned between work and retirement perfectly, and that I would be absolutely ready for the retirement lifestyle. But just four days later, five weeks short of my sixty-ninth birthday and having worked in New York City for fifty years, I was at wit's end—totally trapped, ineffective and feeling like my life was ending.

Over the last fifteen years, we had developed a small farmhouse on ten acres of San Miguel de Allende (SMA) countryside into a gated estate with two houses, two swimming pools, horse stables, a riding arena, myriads of gardens and many fruit and olive trees, all managed by an able family of three; its every cost had been properly projected and well covered within our retirement plan. This is what retirement is all about!

Given all that, one would think I would be very happy, but in reality I was bored; within days after June 30, I was already missing the activities involved in full-time work, as well as its related amenities (meetings, professional relationships, constantly changing environments, etc.). I had no hobbies or pastimes and no one I considered a very close friend to pal around with.

More importantly, I realized that I did not want to live in Mexico, even though we had owned our property there for nearly fifteen years and had made extensive investments to prepare it for retirement. I was in a state of deep depression, but had few options, since we had meticulously consolidated our entire lives into retirement in Mexico. As a result, I felt that I had made a major mistake from which I could not extricate myself; I missed my daughters, my grandchildren and especially living in the United States. Although I had spent the last forty-five years of my advertising career traveling to all the continents, on average, I was flying at least every eight weeks on international assignments. In the end I had always returned home to the US. But not this time, this was a one-way trip to a house in a foreign country.

As I recounted in *The Light of the Serene Moon*, I desperately wanted out, but I accepted our realtor's assessment that selling our place was not going to be easy; the market was limited, and not many people wanted to live in the Mexican countryside. Moreover, Susan was not keen on giving up something that she had created and enjoyed, especially since she had lived there alone for the last five years.

The realtor then suggested that while we waited for a potential buyer, we should consider using agri-tourism to generate income from our property and possibly create a positive selling point for a potential buyer. Since at this point I was grasping at straws and had nothing better to do, I took the advice, drafting a business plan that I eventually shared with Susan, and together we refined it into a plan almost sixty pages long.

My personal objective was unchanged. I wanted out of Mexico, and I was very clear about this with Susan. While she did not object to my attitude, and at times was even supportive, I always felt that she never accepted the idea of willingly leaving Mexico herself.

Our new strategy was to make our Mexican property financially self-sufficient over a three-year period. We also agreed to set aside funds for living expenses and any major investments we considered necessary as our plan evolved. There were three possible outcomes:

> 1. The property would be sold before the plan was finished.
> 2. The plan would be completed successfully, and the financially self-sufficient property would free up funds for another home in the US.
> 3. We would not achieve our plan in three years, in which case we would have a fire sale and unload the property for whatever we could get, then move back to the US.

The planning process would be constantly revised as our plans were adjusted for unforeseen events.

Fortunately, most of these events were positive. Although many such adjustments were made over the course of our plan, we did not waver from the following overall objective and approach.

To apply our investments, learning and experience to create an income-generating enterprise, which can sustain current Mexican operations indefinitely by:

- *Progressively building to achieve an annual net income level by the beginning 2018 that would pay all expenses in Mexico*
- *Expanding our experiences and lifestyles*
- *Expanding and improving the lives of our staff*
- *Dramatically improving our health and well-being*
- *Have fun*

The Approach we would take to achieve the objective was to be:

- *Build a rental business from Mexican properties*
- *Develop a line of farm products to take to market*
- *Record experience for potential publishing*

We considered this the perfect win-win for Susan and me. Fully committing myself to developing a business would keep me engaged and occupied; this was what I had done for almost my entire professional life and had become second nature to me. Susan felt it was a fair approach; there was a good chance that our property would become financially self-sustained, which would give us lifestyle options in the future and for me, this would include flying the Mexican coop!

Our planning continued to evolve during the second half of July. We were invited to attend a vendimia (traditional festival celebrating the grape harvest) at a local winery, where our good friend Gil Gutierrez would be playing with his group of musicians. It was to be held on August 16, which is my birthday; Susan and I decided to see whether we could reserve a table for about twenty people at the event and bring some friends along to celebrate. The winery was only fifteen minutes from our house, so we went to inquire about seating for our group. When we met the owners of the winery, we instantly bonded with them; the four of us spent a wonderful afternoon sitting under a huge mesquite tree and drinking three bottles of their best wine accompanied by cheeses made in a neighboring farm. Everything was set up for my birthday party, and we got in our car and headed home. After all that wine, it was a good thing we were driving a short distance with no traffic!

Susan and I had visited Napa Valley, California, just six weeks earlier. While there, we traveled around the Napa countryside and visited some wineries. We were also interested in olive oil, but it was not something we thought we would ever do, though we did buy some oils and watched a video of the complex equipment required to make it; the process was fascinating, but seemed beyond our capability.

Our winery friends had told us that the state in which we lived was providing strong incentives for the development of wineries. Indeed, we became aware that we had at least three wineries nearby and that many more grapevine fields were being planted. The authorities had even installed large, blue road signs indicating we were in the middle of the "Wine Route."

On one afternoon in the middle of July, we were sitting on our terrace in SMA and contemplating our plan; as we opened a bottle of wine, we remembered that in Napa, wine and olive oil were marketed to the same clientele and the businesses supported each other. I turned to Susan and said, "Hey, why don't we make olive oil and olive products the focus of our agribusiness?"

She gave me a big smile and said, "But of course. I always wanted to do that."

Susan is very reserved in her comments, gestures and facial expressions. I had heard her say, "I always wanted to do that" only on rare occasions; each time, I had taken the bait and launched heart and soul into one of our crazy escapades, and this was no exception: I was hooked, again! Some of our best decisions had been made after a few glasses of wine; I was hoping this was one of them.

A week earlier, we had taken a two-hour ride to a tree nursery in Silao, near the León airport, to replace two trees that had died in our olive grove. It had been at this nursery that our education about types of olives had begun. While there, I had spied a small, squat olive tree with olives bunched as if they were grapes on a vine; when we asked about this variety of olive, we were told that it is an oil olive called "Arbequina." I had purchased three "Arbequina" trees at approximately one hundred seventy dollars each, as well as the two "Manzanilla" trees that we needed, which we had learned is primarily used as a table olive that is cured and eaten. Susan had been curing our olives for the last seven years, but we had had no idea what they are called.

And so two foolhardy New Yorkers, who had just learned that oil olives are used to make olive oil and had only three brand-new oil-olive trees, decided as they were enjoying a few glasses of wine on their terrace that they were going to start making the oil!

Immediately, I began reading every book I could buy or download that discusses olive growing and making olive oil; it quickly became evident that we would have to make a major investment in equipment, trees and labor. Revisiting our plans, we made the necessary adjustments to reflect that we would be making and selling not only olive oil but also olive products. Since we wanted to find out whether we could make olive oil before we spent a lot of money on olive trees and equipment, we needed an olive supplier while our trees developed over a three-year period. We also needed to find bottles, labels and professional support from attorneys and accountants who understand local laws. I was in my element; developing and executing plans and strategies had been part of my profession. An incremental plan was laid out in complete detail covering a three-year period.

Olives have been domesticated, cured and pressed for nearly six thousand years; based on the books I had read, I felt confident that we too could make olive oil. First, we ordered a small press from California.

However, our supply of olives was limited because we did not have enough trees; within weeks, we would resolve both these issues. Meeting the owner of a local tree nursery opened the first of many doors. We purchased our first batch of one hundred thirty small "Arbequina" trees, a Spanish variety widely planted for making olive oil, and we expected to begin producing olives by the third year. The owner of the nursery also gave me the name of someone I could call regarding an olive growers' association that was being formed in our state (Guanajuato); since Susan had already obtained her permanent residency, she became a founding member of the association within a week, so that we were officially established as olive growers. Soon we would have over two hundred trees planted!

Afterward, I was told that the nearby state of Hidalgo had some olive-growing regions as well. This was also the state where the breeder who had sold us our full-bred Dorper sheep (which we had named Ani and Versario) lived; we had an open invitation to visit him, and before the month was over we were on our way.

Previously, I had not traveled much in Mexico during the summer months; my only road trip there had been in December 2005. This trip was different; my eyes were focused on my surroundings because I was not distracted by the needs of a job in New York. As we drove to our host's ranch in Pachuca, I stared at the beauty of the green mountains in Hidalgo, watching sheep graze on the tall grass and feeling the cool mountain air; to me, this did not feel like Mexico at all! I enjoyed our trip, but soon we were heading home.

We had found no olives, but I had discovered something new about Mexico that confused me; prior to this trip, my view of Mexico had been that it is hot, dusty, unclean and full of summer thunderstorms. Arriving back in SMA, I realized our place was just as beautiful as Hidalgo; our horses and sheep were grazing in similar tall grass, and we also breathed wonderful cool mountain air; I was suddenly appreciating all this because I was no longer preoccupied with New York or work. I noticed as well that the seasons in Mexico closely resemble the ones I was used to in New York; during wintertime in the Northeast, the leafless trees make the entire area appear as though it has burned down if it is not snow covered, and in our state of Guanajuato, everything similarly looks dry, yellowish brown and a bit lifeless in winter. After seeing that summers in New York and Guanajuato are both full of beautiful green mountains, I began to think I might be finally adjusting to Mexico.

When we returned home from the trip to Hidalgo

during the last week in July, I started taking pictures to record the developments at our place, like Susan had done daily to keep me informed of what was going on at the farm after she had moved to Mexico in 2009. I was amazed by what I was capturing with the camera on my phone; the farm was producing lots of lemons, limes, peaches, apples, pears, pomegranates, guava, beans, lettuce, corn, garlic, eggs and even sheep.

For part of our research, we went to a store in SMA that specialized in selling olive oil. It looked spectacular; we were impressed with the layout and the displays. After purchasing some bottles of oil and several vinegars, we left with the impression that we would eventually have to be at least as good as this store.

But the biggest surprise of this month was yet to come; at ten o'clock in the morning on July 30, I received a call from a member of the olive growers' association, who said that an olive grower in Hidalgo was having a special event that day. The grower had been funded by the government and would be dedicating a new facility for the processing and warehousing of olive products; the event would take place at two o'clock that afternoon, and since the association member could not make it, he asked whether I would like to go in his stead. I jumped at the chance, and very quickly Susan and I were on another road trip guided by our GPS, as well as my iPad and phone, using some rudimentary directions.

We had no idea where we were heading, but we are

seasoned road-trippers; just six weeks earlier, we had finished a ten-thousand-mile car trip from SMA to Georgia, Florida, Texas, Colorado, Montana, Washington, California, the Grand Canyon and back home, mostly on superhighways. However, the Mexican roads on which we were traveling gradually narrowed, which exasperated us because we were trying to reach our destination by two o'clock, and the GPS directions to the town indicated that we would arrive fifteen minutes late; moreover, we encountered heavy commercial traffic, such as double-trailer rigs going five miles per hour on the mountain roads with only one lane for each way, so that passing these rigs was necessary, but extremely dangerous!

As the GPS displayed that we were approaching our destination, the traffic disappeared, the road became even narrower and we started to climb nearly two thousand feet toward barren, rocky mountain peaks. Arriving at the town, we stopped at an intersection. Painted on the side of a concrete bus shelter was a blue Star of David crowned with an olive leaf and surrounded by the name of the town. Susan and I smiled at each other; we had stumbled upon what we had been looking for weeks earlier. I had read that many years ago, a Jewish organization had donated over fifteen thousand olive trees to people living in the countryside, who have been harvesting the olives ever since; when we had visited our sheep breeder in Pachuca, we had been very disappointed after taking an unsuccessful four-hour side trip to find this area. The small, beautiful village had clean, well-cared-for buildings, and trees loaded with olives were in every yard, even the schoolyards.

Taking our eyes off the trees, we looked around and did not see a single soul in the streets; I panicked, as our strategy once we got there had been to reach our destination the old Mexican way by asking somebody for directions, and there was no one around, including dogs, cats or chickens. The town was totally empty! Then I recalled my friend's instructions: "When you get to the school, make a right." By sheer luck, I remembered this at the exact moment we were by a school, but we had seen several schools. Was this the right school? Or even the right town? When I made the turn, my heart sank; after fifty feet, the pavement turned into a dirt road. I wanted to turn back, but Susan said no; she had spotted a commercial greenhouse ahead and told me to press on. We discovered that we were indeed in the middle of a nursery surrounded by large olive groves. Having owned a nursery in Florida, we knew that even if we missed the event, we had already found our objective.

After driving another three hundred yards down the dirt road, we came upon a well-paved road. Susan said, "What the heck, let's keep on exploring," so we made a left turn around a bend that led to a brand-new building surrounded by greenhouses, screen houses (which are used for commercial growing operations) and lots of cars parked wherever there was a space. A huge green-and-white circus-like tent next to the building seemed to indicate that we were at the right place, so we parked and approached the tent; it had no walls but only a canopy, and underneath were approximately four hundred people dressed in their Sunday best, standing very quietly with their hats off and heads bowed. We walked in and stood by the perimeter, bowing our heads as a priest said a prayer and gave the benediction; the ceremony was starting.

For the next hour, we listened as city, state and federal dignitaries gave speeches and accolades to the community; then came the ribbon-cutting ceremony. It seemed that as usual, we were right where all the action was; we had been standing with our backs to a huge doorway into the building without noticing the ribbon next to us. As the dignitaries left the dais, they started heading in our direction with everyone following them, so that we found ourselves in the middle of the crowd, participating in the congratulations, handshakes and hugs that people were giving each other.

Prior to the ribbon cutting and during the speeches, I had been standing next to a tanned, petite woman wearing jeans and a shirt with the same logo that some of the speakers wore. I had introduced myself, and she had told me that her name was Julia and that she worked with the local growers' association. When I had asked whether the association would sell me olives, she had said yes, given me her phone number and told me to call the following week.

Julia, Susan and I immediately hit it off, and when the

ribbon cutting was over she gave us a tour of the building and all its installations. After the tour, she invited us to lunch with the group, but it was nearly five o'clock, and we knew from experience that we had to leave if we wanted to arrive home by nightfall.

As we drove home that day, we were full of hope and dreams for the future. What a month! We had started it feeling confused about what to do and ended it with clear goals and new connections.
Susan and I like to say, "God takes care of idiots—and we are glad because he takes care of us, and we need a lot of care!"

Making Our First Olive Oil: August 2014

By the beginning of August, our plan was starting to take shape. I was back to working nearly seventy hours per week; I would get up every morning at six thirty, shower, dress, have coffee and breakfast with Susan and be in my office at the cottage by eight o'clock, spending an average of three or four hours at the office and the rest of the time running errands or working with Susan and the staff.

First, we met with Transito (our live-in manager, caretaker and jack-of-all-trades for the last fifteen years, who is also head of his family) and informed him that we planned to go into agri-tourism by making our farm a fun and interesting destination for people to visit. He gave us a perplexed look, but reacted positively; I am sure he thought something like, "What the heck, I'll just follow whatever these *gringos* are doing and see what happens." I further explained that the ultimate goal was to make the farm generate enough income to pay for itself by 2018; this he fully understood, and he wholeheartedly agreed. To summarize our vision, I told him, "In three years, this place is going to look like a park, generate income from rental of the cottage, have a store selling olive products, and we are going to be making olive oil!" Transito immediately took to the tasks involved in making this a reality.

Typically, fruit trees suffer a little when transplanted, and we expected our recently planted "Arbequina" trees to lose fruit and leaves. We were delighted when they did not drop their olives and continued to flourish; the olives were ready for picking by the beginning of August.

But then a different roadblock got in the way; the press we had ordered from the US was delayed in customs. Frustrated that we did not know when it would arrive and driven by our eagerness to make olive oil, we researched how to make our own press; after several days of looking at rope-driven methods and other contraptions, I called Transito and sketched what I thought would work. Over the last fifteen years, we had made a substantial investment in equipment for his workshop; we had welding equipment, a compressor and many different kinds of power and hand tools. We also had suppliers of construction materials that would deliver to our house; Transito ordered the steel he felt we would need and began building our own hydraulic press with heavy-duty steel frames to absorb the pressure we would be exerting to squeeze the juice out of the olives.

On August 6, we loaded a *cubeta* (five-gallon pail) with about thirty pounds of olives from our trees to serve as our first test in making olive oil. From our reading, we knew that our first step was to wash the olives, then crush them, including the pits; we considered various methods and finally agreed that using a manual meat grinder would be our initial approach. Susan was excited; she had her grandmother's meat grinder, so we thought we were in business.

We quickly found out how hard this was going to be; within less than an hour, we stopped using the manual meat grinder because we knew that it would take longer than a day to crush all the olives with it, switching to our KitchenAid mixer with a meat grinder attachment instead. When we had crushed our olives, the next step was to malax (gently stir) the mash to help the oil molecules emulsify (unite) in order to form the olive oil. Afterward, the mashed olives were pressed to force out a juice containing oil and water. Next the oil and water were separated, and finally the oil was filtered to remove any remaining large particles of olives.

After seven hours of work, Susan and I were exhausted. Our thirty pounds of olives had been converted into about a quart and a half of oil; the final product was cloudy and yellowish green with an unfamiliar smell. When we had worked up the nerve to try the stuff, we each grabbed a tablespoon, brought a brimming spoonful to our mouths and swallowed. Immediately, our eyes bulged and began watering, and we coughed like crazy; we thought we would soon be very sick, but to our amazement we adjusted quickly until both the watering and the coughing stopped. We looked at each other and had the same thought: this was the worst stuff we had ever tasted, so we should resort to the first-aid kit—the tequila bottle! Having poured ourselves two full shots as usual, we gently sipped our tequila for the next forty-five minutes, discussing the events of the day and their disappointing outcome; our plan of agri-tourism based on olive products seemed to float away. As we went to bed, we resolved to figure all this out tomorrow.

I often do not sleep straight through the night, and many years ago I had learned that the easiest way to go back to sleep is to grab a book and read a few pages, so when I woke during that night I picked up my phone to read the section of the e-book I had just started that discusses the tasting and effects of olive oil; I read more than the usual number of pages.

In the morning, I told Susan that there was nothing wrong with our olive oil; we were simply experiencing the effects of the polyphenols, antioxidants and anti-inflammatory chemicals in the oil. Fresh olive oil feels rough on the throat and causes the eyes to water, but if one knows to expect those things, the oil can be savored as one appreciates the explosion of different tastes. And so, before our morning coffee, we filled our tablespoons with the olive oil and repeated what we did the previous night; again our eyes watered, and we coughed and felt the burning sensation on our throats, but this time we focused on the tastes we were experiencing: almonds and other nuts, as well as green grass. I was excited—this was exactly what the book had described! It was a wonderfully reassuring feeling.

Since we had proven that we could make olive oil, we were ready to start procuring lots of olives in order to make and sell the oil and other olive products. We needed to establish our brand and our company; more importantly, we also needed to invest in olive trees and to prepare the land and an irrigation system for them. There was quite a bit of work to be done.

I called Julia, and she told us that the oil olives were not ready, but only the "Manzanilla" table olives, which she said are not good for oil because their oil content is less than ten percent, meaning the olives will deliver below ten percent of their weight in oil; I replied that we would buy them anyway, since we were learning to make oil and adjusting our equipment, and therefore making oil from them would still be worthwhile. We drove to Hidalgo more calmly this time; arriving at midday, we had a long discussion with Julia about the process of making olive oil in her community. When I asked what was used for bottles, she said the people came with their own bottles for her to fill. Afterward, we purchased some oil and about four hundred pounds of olives, and soon our foyer was full of olives.

On August 8, we began our day at seven o'clock in the morning, full of hope and eager to start making olive oil. By midday, our KitchenAid mixer had burned out; we had no choice but to look for another one at Liverpool, a nearby department store. There we purchased a more powerful KitchenAid mixer, and fortunately all the attachments we had accumulated over the years fit the new mixer perfectly.

While driving from the store, Susan and I evaluated our

system. The mixer had been doing double duty, grinding the olives and then malaxing them prior to pressing. We thought about the process Julia had shown us; she had an electric motor that rotated a paddle inside a *cubeta*. This motor was identical to the one that drove the blade of our old-fashioned ice-cream maker (an appliance that Susan had brought from Florida and we had not used in Mexico).

Returning to the house with our new mixer, Susan went back to crushing olives; meanwhile, I went directly to one of our storage rooms and located the ice-cream machine and its motor. Then I walked to Transito's workshop and asked him to create a paddle for the motor that would fit into a *cubeta* and be used as a mixer. Transito went to work on this task, and I came back into the house to help Susan crush the olives; less than an hour later, Transito brought our new "malaxer," which allowed us to complete this step of the process much faster.

At this point, a different issue became apparent; the press was slowing us down. At the spur of the moment, I walked back to the workshop and asked Transito to build us another press. That night, we finished making oil at around eight o'clock, but our kitchen and equipment then had to be cleaned, which took us nearly two hours. We had worked all day, not even stopping for lunch or supper, and decided to go to bed. As we passed the foyer, we realized that we had hardly put a dent in the pile of olives! Olives should be processed within forty-eight hours of picking in order to produce extra-virgin oil, and we were well past that mark.

Early on Saturday morning, Transito brought the second press, which worked fine and immediately increased our output; we had finished processing all the olives by Sunday night. Our equipment was not perfect, but it was getting the job done, and we calculated that we were processing more than two hundred pounds of olives per day. As expected, our oil production was not very good, only about two gallons of oil; though we had successfully separated the oil from the water, the oil was also very cloudy (at the time, we incorrectly believed that it should come out clear, just like store-bought oil).

Susan and I began working on separate fronts to tackle the remaining obstacles or tasks. On Monday morning, she focused on securing bottles, jars and *cubetas*, quickly finding a supplier that could provide everything except the bottles. I called Julia to ask for more olives, and she said we could come the next day.

During a short break, Susan and I looked at each other's hands and started laughing; our fingernails were outlined in black because we had been working without gloves. We then tried very hard to wash them clean, but when the effort proved futile, we shrugged it off as a small price to pay for what we were creating; however, we did start wearing gloves. Our hands did not look normal again until about two weeks later.

Concerned that we would burn out the KitchenAid mixer again, we went into town looking for a professional-grade meat grinder. SMA is a town with many, many restaurants; fortunately, we found a store that sold restaurant appliances across the street from our favorite grocery store. When we walked in and looked at the store's shelves, we spotted the same meat grinder we had seen on the Internet while researching oil making; even though it cost nearly a thousand dollars, we bought it.

On Tuesday, Transito and I drove his truck to pick up the olives, which gave us an opportunity to talk; he was getting very excited and motivated to advance our oil-production project. As we neared our destination, I knew we needed to stop somewhere for Transito to have lunch; I had learned from experience that his entire family's biological clock always says, "If it is twelve o'clock, it's time to eat."

I spotted a *barbacoa* place, and we pulled in and parked. Though it was a typical Mexican roadside eatery, it was rather large, about one thousand two hundred square feet, with the usual cheap molded-plastic tables and chairs; the walls and ceiling were tarps. As we entered, a man was chopping some cooked meat on a wooden block and a woman was busy making tortillas; a few very large pots were cooking on a stove near the man.

We sat, and the waitress came to take our order; Transito ordered six tacos and a consommé, and I ordered four tacos and the consommé, though I had no idea what I had just ordered. While I had seen many of these *barbacoa* places throughout my years, I had always thought they were just barbecue places. I asked Transito, "What kind of tacos are we getting?"

"*Barbacoa*," he answered.

"What kind of *barbacoa*?"

"*Borrego*."

So, I was going to have lamb tacos; I asked what kind of consommé, and again he answered, "*Borrego*." I knew then that I was screwed; I had acquired a taste for lamb a few years ago, but rack of lamb and sometimes a well-prepared leg of lamb were as far as I would go. After ordering a Diet Coke, I waited somewhat nervously.

Soon, the waitress returned with two plates and two bowls. I watched Transito as he opened one taco, and it was just a tortilla with a small serving of the meat the man had been chopping, which looked as if it had been boiled, shredded and chopped; I also opened one taco. Transito then reached for the various bowls of condiments, adding onion and cilantro to his taco; I did the same. Next he grabbed a piece of lime and squeezed the juice onto his taco; again I copied him. When he heaped a spoonful of one of the two sauces onto his taco, I knew better than to follow his lead; I used a fork to taste each sauce and decided that the one he had chosen was too spicy for me, so I put a modest spoonful of the other one onto my taco.

He then took a big bite of his taco; I nibbled mine at first, but soon was heartily munching on the delicious taco. All the tacos were quickly eaten. The consommé was a soup containing chickpeas, zucchini, onions and sweet peppers; of course, one added the condiments to taste. Transito felt good, and I was stuffed! Afterward, he said these tacos were okay, but the ones sold near us were much better. I had been unaware of a *barbacoa* place just minutes from our house, so I stored this information in the back of my mind.

We got back in the truck and reached our destination in about thirty minutes. This time, I took my time looking at the tree stock in the nursery; there were quite a few varieties and sizes. I made mental notes and knew I would be coming back for some trees; soon thereafter, we were heading home with another five hundred pounds of "Manzanilla" olives.

Our second week of processing went much faster; we were operating two presses, and María (Transito's wife) and Rosa (one of his daughters) started helping. When we finished processing by Friday evening at five o'clock, we had about six gallons of olive oil. During the last two weeks, we had been operating out of our kitchen and an outdoor cooking area adjacent to the kitchen.

Transito approached me with a family problem. His son, Juan, had been working for us from the beginning of December until around the end of February during each of the last two years; for the rest of the years, he had worked in construction. A common but illegal practice in that industry is to fire the lower-level workers just before the employer is legally required to pay their *aguinaldos* (annual Christmas bonuses), which is equivalent to two weeks' pay for each employee; we had hired Juan during his forced "vacations," since Juan is very good at construction and can build just about anything we need. This time, however, the problem was a little different; as Transito explained it, Juan had been hired by a relative of Transito's, but was paid the lowest salary and was being asked to help offset the gasoline expenses incurred on the way to and from work.

Transito and I agreed that Juan was being abused. I immediately asked Transito to go to Juan's work site (it was Monday morning) and bring him so he can work for us full time; María and Rosa had mostly been caring for the gardens and the trees, but since they would soon be busy making products for market, we needed someone to take up some of these duties. Juan happily joined us.

Saturday, August 16 was a memorable day; we moved the processing operation from our house to the cottage, where Transito and his family took over and processed about a hundred pounds of oil olives picked from our "Arbequina" trees. The oil was amazing! "Arbequina" olives did indeed yield substantially more oil than "Manzanilla" olives, so we decided that we would no longer use the "Manzanilla" olives to produce oil. We also learned that Transito and his family were much better at making the oil than we were; since their steady workflow and attention to detail resulted in a far superior product, we delegated the task to them.

At midday, Transito and his entire family sang happy birthday to me, and we had a wonderful hamburger/hot dog cookout under the shade of the eucalyptus trees. Then, in the late afternoon, we dressed and headed to our new friends' winery to attend the vendimia.

When we arrived, we were given a full tour; during our first visit, we had not made it past the mesquite tree. This time, we were shown the screen house where grape plants were started. Outside the screen house was a large number of ugly, scraggly olive trees in huge containers; I asked about them and was told that the owners' original plan had been to plant olive trees, but their area was too cold and so they had decided to plant grapes instead. The trees were over eight years old and had been imported from California; they were of two varieties, "Mission" and "Arbequina." There were no immediate plans to plant them, so I said, "Give me a good price and I will take them all." I was very serious; Susan and I had quite a bit of experience growing trees in Florida, and we suspected that the eight-year-old unplanted trees had strong root systems and would start yielding fruit within a short time when given the proper care. We then proceeded to the festivities, where we had a wonderful party with a small group of friends in the midst of the other four hundred people.

During the following week, we ordered food-grade *cubetas* with lids, which we used for brine curing six hundred pounds of olives from our trees. This was a familiar process that we knew would take time; the olives first had to be hand picked and sorted, then they were cured in brine for many months. At the same time, we negotiated a deal for the trees at the winery and started to plant the first batch of what would amount to four hundred trees. I was very happy that I had hired Juan; he and his father immediately began planting the trees.

One-third of our property (almost four acres) had been totally pristine; the horses were taken there daily to roam and forage. I was concerned about snakes and other critters living in the tall grass, so our plan called for creating a park atmosphere in this area that would support a new olive grove, yet preserve as many of the natural trees and cacti (*nopales*) as possible. Transito did not readily accept this decision, but I insisted and eventually he came to appreciate how everything seemed to be balanced; two years later, he would truly fall in love with this space and feel proud of his achievement. We have had no problems with snakes or other creatures ever since; I think the increased activity on the land may have scared them off.

On August 25, we started a trip to New York City; my nephew was to be married on Labor Day weekend in

New Jersey. Afterward, we would go down to babysit my grandchildren in Atlanta, Georgia, to which I was really looking forward.

Our base in New York City was with Susan's mother, Grace; as her name implies, she is a graceful woman, ninety-five years young at the time. The first thing we did once we arrived was go to a nail salon for a thorough manicure. We were the talk of the shop; our hands looked worse than a coal miner's, but the black olive stains were finally eliminated. Another hectic month ended with wonderful experiences, great olive oil and clean hands at last.

Making New Friends: September 2014

We returned to SMA on September 11, 2014. After greeting everyone, our first order of business was to test our new press from California. When we quickly realized that our homemade presses were far more effective, Transito immediately began to make two more presses; we needed to increase our production as more olives became available.

Walking around the property, I noticed the peaches and apples were ripening and going to waste as usual, so I visited Susan in her office and obtained her consent to add homemade apple cider to our product offerings; I had a crazy idea that someday we would sell cinnamon doughnuts and apple cider to our visitors. This idea had come from a small roadside stand in a New Jersey apple orchard, which had sold apple cider and doughnuts to people who were paying to pick their own apples; through the years, I had seen this little stand grow into a multi-million-dollar operation with a fifteen-thousand-square-foot building, ten cash registers and parking for hundreds of cars. It now focuses on fresh baked goods, vegetables and cheeses, but the famous apple cider and cinnamon doughnuts are still offered in one corner of the complex. While I never wanted our business to be that large, I thought the cinnamon doughnut/apple cider combination would enhance visitors' experience on our farm. Susan was okay with producing cider but not so much with making doughnuts, though she said she was willing to try; she also asked that we use the core, peels and waste pulp to make apple-cider vinegar, and we adjusted our plan to include this product as well.

I did some research on making an apple-cider press and found lots of information, even how to use a washing machine with spikes inside it to press the cider during the spin cycle, but was still at a loss as to the best design. Walking through the grove and looking at the fallen, wasted apples, I saw María and asked her to fill a bucket with apples, bring them to the cottage, then peel and core them. The rest was easy; first using the meat grinder and then one of the presses, we started making apple cider. María and I were the first to taste it; when I asked her opinion, she gave an unforgettable reply: "My, this is really good—and to think for all these years we have been wasting so many apples."

The apple cider was truly delicious, and we were making so much of it that we developed a pasteurizing process and stored the cider in half-gallon Ball jars. Soon, peaches and pears were put through the same cycle, as well as some of the frozen fresh apricots harvested from our trees early in the spring.

We also researched how to make vinegar as Susan had suggested; the biggest problem turned out to be finding the appropriate large containers. Since there is a manufacturer of blown glass in SMA, we went to the factory's store and found clear glass containers that would each hold about five gallons; they were in the shape of a somewhat squat old-fashioned milk bottle with a wide mouth approximately seven inches in diameter. Initially, we bought five of them, but eventually we would use fifteen of these containers for vinegar making.

María started putting the waste from the cider-making process into the glass containers, but quickly ran out of storage space, so we moved the aging apple, pear, peach and apricot vinegars to the horse-tack room. A closet in the cottage was used for storing juices and oil.

By mid-September, it had become evident that we could successfully make olive oil and olive products. In accordance with our plan, we then began to expand our grove, purchasing additional olive trees and planting them. At this point, we knew a bit more about olive trees; not only did we buy more "Arbequina" trees, but we also added two Italian varieties: "Coratina," which is primarily grown in Puglia, and "Frantoio," which is native to Tuscany.

As the pace of our activities began to quicken, we thanked our lucky stars that we had taken the time to write down every detail of our plan. It seemed as if we were making decisions on the fly and spending a lot of money without a great deal of thought, but since we were following our plan, all the decisions were easy; we had analyzed, argued and discussed as many details as possible long before we made any of these choices.

Through Susan's efforts over the years, we had acquired a lot of experience preserving the bounty from our farm, such as cured olives, apple sauce, sauerkraut, green beans, pickles and apricot and peach butters, as well as salsa, tomato sauce and much more. Very soon, this process also started to accelerate.

Space was at a premium, so we took action on several fronts to create more. First, we rearranged the space allocated to our animals, which involved repurposing two horse stalls. By the end of the month, construction of a country store had begun; Juan's knowledge of electrical systems and masonry was most welcome.

Things started moving fast, but there was a method to our madness. The sixty-page business plan we had written in early July outlined a very detailed course of action; everything we were doing was programmed and working as planned. Nonetheless, we knew that an enormous challenge still lay ahead; we had owned and operated a tropical plant and tree nursery in Florida for five years, and this experience had taught us that the hardest part of farming is marketing and selling the product of one's labor.

As a result, we started focusing on the store, our brand and creating olive products before we even had a viable commercial crop. Friends began to taste our olive oil, and the results were rewarding; many of them wanted to buy our oil, but we did not want to sell it until we had stocked our store, not to mention that we still had no bottles or labels. Susan and I worked as a team, meeting each morning to go over our tasks and at the end of every day to report our progress.

One of the key goals in our well-rounded plan was to expand our experiences and lifestyles. We were already having fun with all the agricultural activities, but we also needed to make friends by going out more often. I was not very good at this part; my friend base had consisted of business co-workers and acquaintances, and in Mexico all that was gone. Even though Susan had lived in Mexico for the last five years, she was in the same boat.

To this end, on September 14 we held an impromptu barbecue with some newfound friends, which included the winery owners, Diane and Higinio, as well as twenty other guests. For the debut of what would become our signature dish, Susan and I had purchased six frenched racks of lamb that we had cut into forty-eight individual ribs. Susan had then prepared an olive oil–based marinade with a concoction of spices and soaked the lamb ribs in it for three days. We also had recently purchased a new Kamado grill at Costco in the nearby town of Celaya, and I filled it with charcoal, lit it and started piling on the lamb ribs when the charcoal had burned to embers. When I tasted the first one off the grill, I was soon joined by a couple of friends, who gobbled up the ribs faster than I could cook them; I realized that at this rate, very few other people would get any food! I then asked my munching friends to pass around the ribs, which were a hit with everyone. But we still had more surprises coming; Susan had also ground a leg of lamb into burger patties, and people began to enjoy lamb burgers, grilled chicken and several cases of wine and beer. Looking back on the event, I guess one could say that it was our coming-out party; soon afterward, we were invited to friends' houses and enjoying incredible hospitality and discussions.

The Kamado grill had functioned perfectly, and trying it out had been a new experience; the more I explored its uses, the more I began to like it. Since it can be used as a grill, a smoker or an oven, it did not take long before we were inviting people to sample our pizzas, as well as smoked salmon, turkey and fresh ham, all cooked on the Kamado grill.

Transito and his family took over processing the olives. By the end of the third week of September, we had developed a full-fledged oil-making operation. The operations center moved to the cottage, and I started watching the process, looking for ways to improve it.

When I noticed that some olive oil was naturally floating to the top of the *cubeta* where the crushed olives were held prior to pressing, I asked María to collect a spoonful so I could taste it. She immediately said that I would like it because she had tasted it and found it to be excellent oil. Then she gave me a taste, and it really was great. One day, I was checking on the operation and saw two one-gallon glass jars; the first one contained olive oil that was almost black, and the second held oil that was very light green. I asked María what the difference was, and she said the dark oil was from normal pressing and the light oil was the floating oil she had collected during the week.

By September 24, María had collected almost half a gallon of the light-colored oil, and the family had made nearly nine gallons of the dark oil. I was freaking out; could the stuff we were producing through normal pressing make people sick? To find out, I took a picture of the two jars and sent it to my friend who was making olive oil in Hidalgo; he reassured me, saying that the dark oil was normal and that the other oil must be okay but was not normal. Then I asked María to make sure that the light oil was kept separate and that only we used it. We tried filtering the darker oil, which still tasted fantastic, but it did not clear up much. Over time, we would learn that artisan olive oil is very pulpy, and the sediment eventually settles harmlessly to the bottom of the bottle, leaving a clear, rich color above.

On Mexico's Independence Day (September 16), SMA hosts a big annual celebrations that is well known both nationally and internationally; our town and nearby Dolores Hidalgo are considered the birthplace of Mexican independence. Cinco de Mayo (May 5) is a US tradition, originally begun in California in 1860 to celebrate the Battle of Puebla (considered by many to be a minor battle) and popularized in the 1980s by beer and liquor companies to sell more beverages. Ask most Mexicans about Cinco de Mayo, and they will have no idea what it is; ask them about Independence Day, and they will smile as they say, "*El Grito, Independencia,*

San Miguel de Allende, Dolores Hidalgo, y el 16 de Septiembre!"

Following the Independence Day celebration, SMA holds its annual *Feria* (Fair), which is very similar to a country fair, lasting more than two weeks and is replete with the typical attractions, food and crowds. To this day, we have yet to go to that section of the fair; however, during the last four or five years we have gone to the section where there are competitions for farm animals and where farm equipment (including heavy machinery) is displayed and sold. This was where I had bought Ani and Versario a year earlier.

This September, Gregorio, our sheep-breeder friend, asked whether he, his wife and his cousin could stay at our cottage while they entered their sheep during the four-day competition at the fair; Gregorio usually came with twenty or thirty of his best sheep and took home some prizes. The final day of judging was a major affair and when the prizes were awarded; prior to that, there was a lot of trading, and Gregorio's stay gave us some insight into the trade. In the end, however, we decided that it was just a hobby for us; we did not take it any further.

Our circle of friends was expanding rapidly, and we were being introduced to their magnificent houses, as well as to new eating venues; one of these eateries is very close to our home and located at a place locally known as Hacienda de Landeta. We were already familiar with the location, as a few years ago there had been a very good Italian restaurant in the hacienda that we had frequented whenever I visited SMA. Starting at our property, which is situated near the end of a traffic-less clay road about three miles long, and going toward town, one comes to a blacktop road and reaches Hacienda de Landeta after less than a two-minute ride on the blacktop. Though we do not know how old the hacienda is, the buildings seem to be hundreds of years old and are made of the stones strewn throughout our area.

The space the Italian restaurant had vacated was unoccupied until in September of 2014 it was rented to a red-haired Mexican chef from the Gulf Coast, who opened a restaurant called Rojo Vivo (Bright Red) featuring wood-fire-broiled hamburgers and other meats. We were one of his first customers, and we found the food delicious and very convenient, as we had formed the New York habit of "eating in" (ordering meals to be delivered at home); to this day, when we get that urge we call Rojo and order his burgers and fries. Recently, we have created a rule that we do it only once per month, as it can be addictive and we were consuming too many calories, so that I now keep track of when we order from Rojo.

The next item in our business plan was addressing the issues of a local checking account. For fifteen years, we had lived with Mexico's unique banking laws, which attempted to prevent money laundering within its borders due to the influence of the United States. We suffered through a five-hundred-dollar limit on cash obtained through an ATM, controls on cashing foreign checks, etc.; it seemed that every year there was some new regulation on accessing money.

Since we were setting up a business, we had decided to open a local bank checking account. This is a simple thing to do in the US, but not in Mexico at the time; the paperwork took about three days to process. We opened a joint account in both of our names, but found out later that all the checks and other bank documents show only the husband's name (such chauvinism!), so we opened another account in Susan's name.

But opening the accounts was only half the struggle; trying to access the information online was so exasperating that finally Susan insisted on having a bank executive show her how to do it. As a fun-loving guy, I recorded the event for posterity, taking a few pictures of Susan at the bank as she was getting private lessons from the bank executive. Going to all that trouble was indeed worth it; Susan has become an expert on the electronic transfer of funds to our suppliers, and we have come to like—if not love—the simplicity of the system.

The postal service in Mexico must not very reliable, since to avoid mailing checks the banking system had developed a cyber-network that allows funds to be transferred almost instantaneously from an account in one bank to another account in a different bank. Opening bank accounts did not seem like something we needed at the time; however, as our business grew it became obvious that we could not operate without them.

When I saw the trees from the winery as they were being planted, I started having second thoughts about purchasing them. These were the ugliest, most pathetic trees I had ever seen; some had just a few leaves on them. To compensate for the mistake I had probably made, I began looking for more trees to plant; more importantly, we also implemented a rigorous schedule of watering and fertilization.

As the end of September approached, I began to notice that the trees were losing their leaves; some were almost bare. Upon closer examination, I discovered that most of the area where we had planted new olive trees was infested with leafcutter ants. I knew of one thing I could buy that would kill them, but I also knew the chemical was not organic; we wanted to keep our farm free of non-organic pesticides and herbicides. When I did some Internet research on leafcutter ants and started talking to people about them, I learned these ants are very hardy pests that cut leaves off of trees to feed a fungus, which eventually is fed to their larvae; they also eat the sap of the leaf. If a certain leaf is bad for the fungus, it is also bad for the ants, but they love olive leaves and can strip a large tree of its leaves overnight, which does not kill the tree but stunts its growth for at least a year.

Through my research, I started making various concoctions. First, we tried spraying the trees with a mixture of garlic, jalapeño and onion that seemed to work, but only for a short time; the ants would return as soon as the spray's effects wore off. Next we tried pouring dishwasher detergent mixed with garlic down the entry to their nest; this was also effective for a while, but again the pests kept coming back. We felt like we were losing this battle.

As the month came to a close, we were invited to Mary Ellen and Jordi's home; we had recently met them when they came to our famous barbecue. Mary Ellen was born in Puerto Rico like me and so we had bonded; Jordi was born in Spain and knows a lot about olive oil. Our visit to their house was almost exactly like our barbecue; even the guests were similar.

One of their friends was also the architect who had designed the three-meter-high wall surrounding their custom-built home on more than an acre of land, as well as the property's meticulous and brilliant landscape, including the free-form swimming pool with a cascading waterfall. I was introduced to the architect, whom Susan already knew; later, I asked her how she knew him, and she said he had landscaped our home fourteen years earlier. During my conversation with him, I asked whether he knew an organic way to get rid of leafcutter ants; he blurted out, "Tanglefoot," then explained that it is a product available in the United States that will do the job. Upon returning home from the party, I immediately logged into Amazon.com and ordered a good deal of Tanglefoot.

The Best Olive Oil I Ever Tasted: October 2014

During the get-together at his house, Jordi had given me a tour; we had especially admired his three "Arbequina" trees loaded with olives. I had then invited him to bring his olives to our house so we could press them for olive oil. He took us up on the offer, and he and Mary Ellen came with two *cubetas* full of olives, as well as lots of empty jars. We ground the olives with the meat grinder and began malaxing them in the KitchenAid mixer; I saw that the olive oil was not forming, but I kept this observation to myself. When we pressed the olives, they did not yield the amount of oil that we had expected, but only about a quart; I surmised that the olives had not ripened enough and should have been picked much later. Jordi and Mary Ellen were not disappointed, however; to them, going home with a quart of olive oil produced from their trees was a step in the right direction.

As we neared the end of our task, we fired up the Kamado grill. While the charcoal fire burned to embers, we opened up the first of three bottles of champagne, which was soon accompanied by our famous lamb ribs. Jordi introduced us to *pan con tomate y pan con ajo* (bread with tomato and bread with garlic), toasted bread rubbed with either tomatoes or garlic and smothered in olive oil; during that glorious afternoon, the four of us ate a whole loaf of French bread toasted on the Kamado grill and prepared in this fashion. I became a great admirer of Mary Ellen and Jordi when they told us that they had crossed the Atlantic on a twenty-six-foot boat—what a feat!

Sunday, October 5, 2014, would prove to be a key day in our evolving project. Our very good friends Gil and his wife, Rebecca, began a series of soft openings at the country venue they had built. Once they felt ready, they planned to start a business initially holding music concerts, but in the meantime they invited various friends on Sunday afternoons; we were always invited, and we always accepted the offer.

We had met Gil and Rebecca in 2007, and they had become our best friends, as close as family members. Susan and I had even influenced their two children's decision to start careers in advertising; they both worked in New York City. When I had retired from my New York job after June 30, Gil had been my pal, probably my first one in many years, and we had enjoyed each other's company. Since we have the same last name, he would always jocularly introduce me to friends as his older brother; much later, I found out that some people had begun to believe we were related.

That first event at the venue was even more special because Gil had not only invited many of his close local friends but also assembled an amazing group of musicians, including Doc Severinsen on the trumpet and Camille Garcia on the accordion, as well as a locally well-known keyboard player, Gabriel Hernandez. We had met Doc in 2007 at the same time we met Gil, and had talked quite a few times afterward. Camille and Gabriel had been introduced to us at the vendimia.

We had seen their place grow from an idea to a splendidly designed, well-built venue, though at this point it was not ready for handling public events. Its construction was still unfinished; there was only one bathroom, and another was being built. Also, the electricity to the building was not yet connected, so it was provided by a generator that I had lent to Gil.

Not only was our typical barbecue crowd there, but we also made some new friends: Pablo and Denise from nearby Querétaro, as well as Lisabette and Jamie, who lived in SMA. We all sang and danced from about one o'clock in the afternoon to about ten o'clock in the evening. Gil made a point of letting many people know that we were making olive oil, and it became a point of interest in some of our conversations with people. When these discussions about oil became animated, we knew there was pent-up demand that would require more production, but our olive-pressing capacity was being hindered because our KitchenAid mixer was too small; when we spoke with Pablo about this, he said he would research where we could locate a larger one in Querétaro. A few days later, we met with Pablo and Denise in Querétaro, where we were introduced to several suppliers of restaurant equipment, and by the end of the week our new mixer had been delivered; it was capable of handling fifty pounds of olives at once.

Uncertain of the quality of our olive oil and how well it would be received, we kept looking for opportunities to have knowledgeable people taste it. During the Sunday events at Gil and Rebecca's place, we brought our oil for people to taste. Lisabette and Jamie were particularly helpful, as they had spent quite a few years in Cortona, Italy, and had even picked olives, so they were good judges of olive oil; when they tasted our oil and gave their approval, we knew we were doing something right.

Susan and I began experimenting with new products; I had recently studied how to infuse olive oil with various flavors. Our first attempt was infusing olive oil with rosemary; when we found it was successful, we stored the oil in a two-quart Ball jar. Soon afterward, we were trying out basil, garlic and lemon infusions. Though our storeroom was getting full, we did not make large quantities, as we did not know how well the products would sell; keeping small inventories allowed us to make infused oil at will with ingredients grown on our farm.

While Susan and I were busy ordering supplies, developing our products and planning our marketing and sales strategies, our four employees were not only performing their assigned daily tasks but also doing whatever else was necessary to accomplish our plan. Transito orchestrated all activities on our property outside the houses until the end of the day at five o'clock in the evening, when he would take his family to their house in town spend three or four hours with his children and grandchildren. Between seven and nine in the evening, he returned to our farm and stayed at his comfortable two-bedroom apartment next to the cottage. One of his bedrooms has a convertible sofa, so it doubles as his living room; he has Dish Network, a telephone and all the necessary appliances. Before going to bed, he walked the property to make sure everything was in order. After waking up in the morning, at six thirty he drove to his home less than ten minutes away to pick up María, Rosa and Juan. They all arrived by seven and planned their day while having breakfast together; their routine thereafter varied from day to day. Over the seventeen years they have been with us, we have never seen them raise their voices or argue at all with each other.

Juan's day began with taking the horses and sheep to pasture, then feeding and watering the chickens. Next he spent nearly two hours cleaning out the stalls and paddock area. The rest of his daily routine could include gardening, maintaining the lawns or trimming the hedges. He also led construction projects with Transito's assistance and helped his father with repairs and other projects. At around four thirty in the afternoon, Juan prepared the evening alfalfa feed for the sheep and horses and made sure they had water before he brought the sheep to their pens and the horses to the paddock area.

María and Rosa were in charge of the houses and our seven dogs. Tobi, Transito's dog, is truly a working member of our staff; at night, he stays in his house outside Transito's apartment. As our guard dog, he barks to sound the alarm when he senses anything out of the ordinary, like cars going by our property or animals intruding on his territory (he has been skunked more than once). He reacts to any sound, and on many occasions we have watched him make his rounds on the property. In the morning, he particularly likes taking the sheep to paddock before joining the other dogs; he is absolutely wonderful with all the animals.

Rosa's first task was to feed the dogs. María stripped and made the beds, collected the laundry and was soon joined by Rosa to do laundry and clean the house; all this was normally accomplished by ten thirty in the morning. Their routine then gravitated more toward processing the olives, vinegars and ciders, as well as learning about new recipes and products we assigned to them from time to time. Prior to our project, their duties had also included outdoor chores, but Juan had taken over that work.

At the beginning of October, the Tanglefoot arrived. Juan and Transito first covered a section at least two inches all around the base of each tree trunk with masking tape, then they used a brush to apply the Tanglefoot onto the tape; Tanglefoot is a thick, sticky, waxy substance that prevents anything trying to climb up the tree from going any further. Since at this point we had nearly six hundred trees planted, this was not an easy task, but our staff's patience and steady workflow allowed for its quick completion. As their food source became scarcer, the ants started dwindling and moving away to non-olive-producing areas; while the ants were not completely gone, they were no longer damaging the trees. To keep the ants under control, Transito started patrolling for nests (holes in the ground with powdery soil around them); if he found one, he used bait that would eventually kill the fungus.

Our other key project for Juan and Transito was converting the two stalls for horses into a space for our store. At the rear of each stall was a large entrance that allowed the horses to access their individual stalls at night, thus giving then an indoor sleeping space with a yard outside; I had asked that the two openings be closed and that two windows be installed. Within a couple of days, this task was finished. Through the years, I had been annoyed by Transito's habit of not throwing anything away; he had what I viewed as a large junk pile in one corner of the property. As I looked at the windows that had been installed in this new space, I recognized them; they had been taken out of one the bedrooms when we were expanding it. The store space was looking fantastic; Juan had installed the electrical outlets exactly as I had requested. Next I asked that the walls be power washed to remove the smell and stains that had accumulated over a fifteen-year period. This was very effectively done, and the compressor was then used to spray the interior of the room with white paint. We engaged a local iron artisan to build two doors for the entries to the space, and by the end of October Juan had completed installing its new ceramic tiled floor.

We had become very good friends with Higinio and Diane; during one of their visits, we showed them our progress. When they saw we were making vinegar, they offered to give us fifty cases of organic wine they had received from some one else and that had begun to sour. Accepting the gift, we proceeded to turn the wine into vinegar.

In the middle of the month, it was time for my biannual blood test; I had been diagnosed with diabetes in 2007. After several attempts to treat the disease with traditional drugs that had given me serious adverse effects (I had lost four teeth in three months), with the help of doctors I had begun a rigorous treatment that naturally controlled my diet and exercise; no doctor had been more supportive and knowledgeable throughout this process than my local SMA doctor, Arturo Barrera. My test showed that my diabetes was still totally under control, but there were other positive signs that had not been present before.

A week later, I went to my routine appointment to discuss the results with the doctor. Just as I had expected, when I gave him my results he quickly asked, "What have you been doing?" My total cholesterol level had dropped from 245 to 111, and all my cholesterol components were under control. I told him I was doing the same things as usual except that I also was eating lots of olive oil. When he asked why, I told him I was making olive oil; he then asked where, and I said here at our place in SMA, adding that the oil was very good.

The doctor said that he and his brother had traveled through Italy and that he loved olive oil, but he did not think olives would grow well in SMA, so he asked how I knew my oil was good; I replied that I had bought some very good oils in New York and mine was of the same quality. Upon hearing this, he asked whether he could visit us, and we arranged for him to come on Saturday; he came not only that Saturday but also the next six Saturdays!

Since then, Arturo and his wife, Maga, have also become part of our inner circle of friends. His knowledge and support have been particularly helpful; I will never forget something he said during his first visit that has inspired us throughout our development process: "Most Mexicans believe that certain products must be imported for them to be good because we cannot produce them in Mexico. Your oil is something that will make Mexicans proud." During those early visits, Arturo brought his chef friends as well as his brother and other family members. As the chefs got to know us, they began giving us advice, which later would be instrumental when we introduced our olive oil into the local marketplace.

As our oil production increased, we began looking for a safe storage system. Susan contacted one of our suppliers and we started buying food-grade heavy-duty plastic containers that hold about twenty-two liters each.

Having completed the construction of the store, we began to consider how we would furnish it. Meeting with Transito, we designed a very simple cabinet about eight feet long, two feet deep and three feet high. We made its frame of steel and its sides, doors and top of three-quarter-inch-thick plywood, then painted the steel a rich green color with glossy vinyl base paint; finally, we added a shelf about one foot above the cabinet. As soon as we had finished it, we placed it in the store and started using the storage space within it.

As the month came to a close we needed to take time out to prune the older olive trees. They were getting too tall for making hand picking safe and effective so we did some selective pruning.

Mexico has some very interesting holy days. My most recent favorite is one that I had not paid much attention to until 2014; it is held on November 2 each year and called the Day of the Dead (*el Día de los Muertos*). When I had first begun traveling to Mexico (starting with a business trip to Mexico City in 1970), I had found it very odd to see what had looked to me like some sort of skull worship; I had never liked skulls or skeletons because they had scared me as a little boy, and even as a grown-up they had still freaked me out.

I had finally taken some interest in this tradition when Grace had visited Mexico in 2000 specifically to celebrate the Day of the Dead with Transito and his family; afterward, I had asked what had happened, and she had told me that she had had a wonderful day at the cemetery with them. Then I had done a bit of reading and spoken to Susan about it; as I understand it, Mexicans believe that the dead are still with us, and on November 2 they feast at the cemeteries, where they visit the graves of departed family members and reflect on their memories of those who have passed on.

Roughly a week before the end of October 2014, Susan came home with about seven large potted orange and yellow mums in full bloom, and then she showed up with some candy shaped like skulls and skeletons. A few days later, she was arranging a particular corner of the living room, where she had placed all the flowers and candy, as well as the ashes of our dogs that had passed away, along with their pictures and those of my parents, her father and my nephew, all of whom had also died; I asked what she was doing, and she said that she was preparing her altar for the Day of the Dead. I understood, and for the next several days I communed with and enjoyed my memories of those that had passed from my life; it made me feel good, warm and complete.

The End of Our First Pressing Season: November 2014

I began this month totally frustrated and demoralized because I was unable to obtain the right kind of bottle for olive oil. First, I had contacted the largest glass-bottle manufacturer in Mexico, and immediately I had been brusquely told that if I could not order at least ten thousand bottles at one time, they could not even talk to me. Then I had called people in Italy, Spain and the US, again to no avail.

One company in California had told me that they would be more than happy to not only supply the bottles but also give me expert advice on setting up a store. For a brief period, I had been excited to be getting some real support; according to the information that the company had given me, I would be entitled to an exclusive territory as long as I also purchased the company's oils, vinegars, olives, etc. The company's name, Veronica Foods, had sounded familiar, so I had gone to the pantry and looked at the back of the bottle from the SMA olive-oil shop we had visited; there I had found printed on the bottle that it had been provided by Veronica Foods, as well as the appropriate California phone number. At that moment, I had quickly realized these people could not help me, since they already had a representative in SMA.

Resuming my search, I had found a few solutions outside of Mexico, but they were too expensive and so would not be commercially viable. My anxiety about this problem had been compounded by my desire to bring some oil to our friends and relatives during our upcoming Thanksgiving trip to New York. Finally, I found a supplier in the town of Irapuato, which is a ninety-minute car ride away from our house.

Our drive to Irapuato was very different from the one to Hidalgo. Starting in SMA, we headed in our Ford Escape hybrid toward the town of Celaya on a divided four-lane highway; we were very familiar with this road, as Celaya is where our nearest Costco is located and where we do most of our monthly shopping. After reaching Celaya, for about an hour we traveled free and clear on a superhighway to Irapuato, ranging in speed between seventy and eighty miles per hour.

We were mesmerized by the incredibly large fields of corn and various other major crops planted in the area, but we were truly surprised to see a Honda automobile factory in the middle of it all, especially since we knew one of General Motors' major plants is located in Silao. Apparently, our state of Guanajuato has a strong manufacturing as well as agricultural output; we started to feel like we were living in the Midwest of the US.

Using our three GPS devices, we arrived at a small warehouse that displayed many bottles in a glass case under its counter; unfortunately, most of the samples were older models that this outfit was no longer making. We purchased bottles in several sizes, as well as some jars for olives; the workhorse bottle was to be a two-hundred-fifty-milliliter square one, and we selected a tamper-proof propylene gold-colored cap. In total, we bought four hundred eighty bottles (twenty cases of twenty-four bottles each), though I was dissatisfied with these bottles because most of the literature on olive oil says that it should be packed in dark-colored bottles; I will discuss this later.

Interestingly enough, all three of the GPS units took us through part of the town in a roundabout way to get back on the main highway; on this route, we passed a major stockyard and cattle feedlots.

After arriving home, I gave the bottles to Rosa and asked that a couple of cases be filled with our olive oil.

My education on vinegars and olive oil was accelerating. Over the last four months, I had purchased six books about olive oil and seven about vinegar, and I read every one of them; after all, I was again working more than seventy hours per week, and this time I was doing it for my own business. I even watched a film about making olive oil in Provence that helped me determine what to do with the wastewater and pulp; we started using them to fertilize the olive trees. Other books I read also discussed problems we needed to address, and I slowly became very well acquainted with the entire industry of olive products, from seedlings to consumption; sometimes, however, I still needed to add a little common sense to overcome obstacles.

I also learned that there is a great deal of olive-oil adulteration occurring all over the world; if I recall correctly, a study by one of the major universities in California showed that approximately seventy percent of olive oil found on US store shelves is adulterated. Almost a year later, I watched a CBS "60 Minutes" documentary revealing how canola oil is made to both look and taste like extra-virgin olive oil by adding beta-carotene and chlorophyll and that adulteration has even killed people in Spain and Italy. This is not a conspiracy theory; a simple Google search will lead to articles on some scandalous events that authorities in countries producing olive oil have tried to keep quiet.

Building our own presses was not as easy as I may have made it sound; even after we had constructed and started using the first one, we had tinkered with it to increase its effectiveness. An olive-oil press is a fairly complex piece of machinery with quite a few parts; finding or crafting the various components was difficult, and we often tried out new kinds of filters, screens, discs and hydraulics. Since we never stopped pressing over this four-month period, we gradually achieved more satisfactory results. All these efforts took a lot of investment and thought; consequently, we decided to keep our pressing equipment under lock and key and that our entire process would not be open to the public. Transito and I are always looking for ways to perfect our overall system; whenever time allows, we experiment with metals and other materials, so that we have accumulated a small scrap pile. We know that we have a very good process because we have tasted the same type of olive oil from two competitors that have different equipment, and our oil is by far the superior product.

Our pressing season had ended by the first week of November; things had moved so fast that we could not document them all and therefore can only estimate how many products we made. We cured olives, gave more cider to our friends than we kept and have no record of how much vinegar was started that fall. Since we do know we did not sell our products, we can say for sure that rather than making any money, we spent a lot of money, probably over thirty thousand dollars in just three months, not including our normal operating expenses; however, the funds had been clearly projected in our plan. Here is a list of what we had accomplished thus far:

- We learned how to make olive oil and acquired an inventory that would eventually have a value of six hundred thousand pesos, which at the time was the equivalent of fifty thousand dollars according to the exchange rate of twelve pesos to one dollar.
- We cured three hundred kilograms of olives, which had a value of ninety thousand pesos, or seven thousand five hundred dollars.
- We learned how to make cider.
- We started making vinegar, and though it was fermenting we had no idea how it would turn out.
- We built our own presses.

- We purchased some pretty heavy equipment for grinding and mixing the olives.
- We built a store of approximately four hundred square feet.
- We trained our staff in making our products.
- We made a lot of new friends.
- My cholesterol levels were under control with no medication.

These may not have been clear signs of success, but we were heading in the right direction. Our plan still predicted major hurdles ahead, however, of which the least was finding bottles and the most serious was selling what we had made. As impressive as the above list is, probably the biggest achievement of all was the change in my mental state; I was no longer depressed, had become healthier and as a result was not focusing on selling the place in Mexico, but instead was having fun (our fifth and final goal)!

Life returned to normalcy; Transito continued building cabinets for the store while the rest of the staff carried on with the gardening chores. As usual, the weekends (from Friday to Sunday) were full of invitations to *comida*, a late lunch typically beginning between one and three in the afternoon and ending between five and seven in the evening. Adopting this practice, we started to also invite people over for one of the two weekend days. Once in a while, Gil and his musician friends joined us, so that our great room became like a miniature concert hall. Our *comidas* had three different venues that each seated up to ten people. The roof terrace was preferred unless it was too cold or windy;

the next choices were the dining area on our downstairs terrace and finally our main dining room, which we used for parties that would last into the night. We still enjoy hosting these parties.

The *comidas* were key to achieving two important tasks of our business plan; the first was obviously to meet new friends as part of our goal to improve our lifestyle, and the second was a bit more covert. Part of building a tourism destination was offering our store visitors what I called an eatery, which enabled us to provide potential customers with a simple breakfast, lunch or dinner using most of the foods grown on our farm; in order to accomplish this, we needed to train our staff in cooking something other than Mexican food. Slowly, we began adding entrées to Rosa and María's repertoire when they were cooking for our *comidas*. At first, our version of *frijoles charros* (cowboy beans) was always included, and they also sautéed chayote with onions, tomatoes and garlic in a red sauce; the beans, chayote, onions and garlic all came from our garden, and these two dishes were consistently accompanied by María's red or white rice. Transito rounded out the main course by grilling some good barbecue meats. Once in a while, Susan would throw in a surprise dessert, such as home-baked apple or peach pie with a serving of her homemade ice cream.

Since I was paying closer attention to our surroundings and our farm, I started noticing things that had been there all the time but that my previous negativity about Mexico had not allowed me to see. In mid-November, many of the fruit trees started changing color; the yellow to deep-orange leaves were so striking that I started taking pictures and even making videos of them.

When the sheep began to multiply, we decided to build a movable pen system so we could control where they were fed when we put them out to pasture each day; otherwise, the sheep would eat the leaves and bark from the fruit trees and even the pine trees. Once the pens were in place, the sheep were herded into them; watching them graze became one of my (and the dogs') favorite pastimes.

For most of the month, I was in my office executing our business plan, particularly focusing on how we would market and sell our products. We knew we had to build our brand, but first we needed to name it. After some discussion, we decided that our property's official name would be Finca Luna Serena. In 1999, we had named our place *Rancho Luna Serena*, the Ranch of the Serene Moon, on a night shortly after moving in, when we had been mesmerized by the moonlight through our great room's glass ceiling; as our property had become more of an estate, we had dropped the word *Rancho* and called the main house Villa Luna Serena. Since our place is a farming estate, we selected the Spanish word *finca*, which means "estate"; although it is not widely used in Mexico, it felt appropriate because it is also related to farming.

Then I took the opportunity to design our website during the work lull, registering the domain name fincalunaserena.com and drafting what the pages would look like. I had acquired some basic skills in website development when I had built and maintained a website for our main house, which had been rented several times per year from 2001 to 2009, the period when Susan had not lived at the Mexican house. The hardest part of developing the website for Finca Luna Serena was writing the copy, but I was able to put up something decent by midmonth; however, the website was not yet ready for primetime, so no one knew about it because no one was looking for it.

The Thanksgiving holiday approached, and we were scheduled to leave for New York on November 24. I was very apprehensive; a year earlier, I had canceled a pre-Thanksgiving flight to New York due to very bad chest pains. I had gone to see Dr. Barrera, but I had not been alarmed because I had suspected that my costochondritis (inflammation of the cartilage on the chest cavity) had relapsed. Dr. Barrera had conducted a few tests and a chest x-ray, all of which had confirmed my suspicions. At the time, I had still been working, so I had had responsibilities to fulfill and several meetings to attend in New York. A week after that Thanksgiving, Susan and I had departed SMA by car for New York; on the way, the pains had returned, but I had stayed calm and called my New York cardiologist to make an appointment with him. Upon arriving in New York, I had gone to my appointment, and less than a week later a stent had been placed inside me for a blockage in one of the arteries in my heart.

Over the past twelve months, I had still suffered from pings and pangs in my chest, but I was a feeling a lot better than I had before the procedure; nevertheless, I continued to have chest pains from the costochondritis. As we prepared to depart, I was truly not looking forward to leaving our Mexican nest. Our main reason for going was to celebrate my brother Al's sixtieth birthday; but for this important event, I would not have overcome my anxiety. Dr. Barrera prescribed a mild sedative in case I started becoming neurotic; it gave me a sense of security, but I did not use it.

We flew to New York on the twenty-fourth of November; though it was unnecessary, we prudently stayed at Grace's apartment instead of a fancy hotel, since we were retired with no visible income and therefore no longer enjoying the benefits of a job and its related expense coverage. In any event, I am sure Grace would have made a fuss had we not stayed with her.

The small party for my brother was very special, since for the first time in many years most of our family members from the Northeast were there, totaling twenty people. He had selected a Puerto Rican restaurant, and it turned out to be a nice affair.

Since we did not have enough olive oil for my side of the family, we gave it to Grace so she could share it with her daughter Ruth and friends. Our Thanksgiving dinner at Grace's was fine as usual, but of course we were all enjoying the oil also.

I rented a car for a day, drove to New Jersey and picked up my sister Minerva; during the Easter and Christmas seasons, we always visited our loving parents at a cemetery. My father had passed away at the age of ninety-four in 2001, and my mother had passed away in 2006 at the age of ninety. We purchased a Christmas blanket for our parents' grave and said a few prayers; when we both had the feeling that we would not be back for a while, we also had a good cry.

Within a week, Susan and I headed back to Mexico.

Fitting out the Store: December 2014

Our plan called for the store to be finished by year
three. We had sped up the process after ascertaining
that we could make olive oil and secure a good source
of olives; we wanted to build our brand and a sales
stream before our own trees began strong production,
which we estimated would be in 2018 based on what
we had read. When we arrived from our trip, Transito
was busy installing the store's two metal doors, which
we had ordered from our local ironworker. The glazier
who did all of our glasswork then installed the glass for
the doors. In addition, a second cabinet was being
constructed for the store.

Susan ordered some vinegar-testing equipment that
would aid in determining acid levels. She had taken
over the task of learning about vinegars and developing
our process.

Meanwhile, I started designing our logo. We had always
incorporated moons into our names, and therefore I
had to have one in our logo; I could quickly find only
one in the public domain that was somewhat
applicable, a large yellow moon with a desert scene and
cacti in the foreground, so I settled for that and
downloaded it to the computer program I was using to
make the logo. The rest of the logo was very simple; I
added more black space under the moon, where the
copy read "Finca Luna Serena" in large yellow letters

and "San Miguel de Allende, Guanajuato, Mexico" in a smaller yellow font below. I then put the file on a thumb drive.

Next Susan and I headed to the Office Depot store where we planned to have the labels printed. Upon arriving there, we handed the thumb drive to the clerk, who downloaded the file to his computer, then promptly told us that the file was incompatible with the operating system. After he had given us instructions on how to convert the file into a different format, we went back to the house, reformatted the file and returned to Office Depot. The file was fine this time, and we selected a special plastic-coated paper appropriate for a bottle that would contain oil; the clerk told us that we would have to cut each individual label from a sheet containing about fifty labels.

We came home and proudly went into our store to put the labels on our olive-oil bottles. Cutting each label was not a problem, but removing the paper from the back of the plastic so we could affix the label to a bottle proved almost impossible. Our labels gave no indication as to the contents of the bottles, so at Office Depot we had also obtained small plain white printable adhesive labels in sheets of one hundred per page; we planned to print the names of our products on the sheets and then apply a sticker on each bottle just below the moon label.

Our main competitor, the local olive-oil store, was using fustis (Italian stainless-steel containers) that each held a different type of olive oil; customers would select the oil they wanted, which would then be poured from the corresponding fusti into a bottle and sealed while they watched. Though we wanted to copy this system, we considered the fustis too expensive; we did not even know where to buy them in Mexico, and getting them from Amazon.com in the US would cost almost two hundred fifty dollars apiece. More importantly, we planned to design our store in a Mexican style, and fustis would not have the right look. I remembered reading in one of my books that the ancient Greeks and Romans transported their olive oil in large clay urns, so we decided upon a locally produced talavera jug with a spout, which normally dispenses water; these jugs, called *garrafóns*, are common in Mexico and made of clay with a very durable high-fired porcelain layer inside and out that is hand painted before being baked onto the jug and can be very beautiful. We drove to a talavera factory, consulted the owners and came home with six jugs that we would fill with natural olive oil as well as infused oils.

As the store was being completed, I kept staring at the ceiling; it was finished in a corrugated sheet metal that one would typically find in a horse stall. This looked terrible and did not support the ambience we were trying to create. I recalled that the large barn that had been converted into an events hall at Dos Buhos, a nearby winery, had a hanging material covering the lamina on its ceiling, so we decided to use the same method. We then drove to a store called Parisina that sells many varieties of fabrics, where we bought nearly five hundred square feet of an inexpensive cream-colored material resembling rough linen.

Bringing the fabric to María, we asked her to cut it into five-meter lengths and hem each edge; the resulting panels would be approximately two meters wide and five meters long. She finished this on the following day. Since we had some spare copper piping lying around from a defunct project, I requested that it be painted the same green we were using on the metal frames for the furniture; the pipe would serve as the central hanger across the length of the room. Next the line that would hold the panels up was fitted through the hanger, and we threaded heavy-duty wire though the hems against the walls, which we then fastened with very strong masonry nails. Each panel of material was hung across the width of the room from the wall to the center, drooping about eight inches below the lamina on both sides of the hanger; the transformation of the ceiling enhanced the look and feel of the store, exactly as we had envisioned.

Getting ready for the Christmas season, we had bought our tree and unpacked the dog costumes and tree decorations by the first week in December. The costumes were only for Simba, our oldest dog, a mutt resembling a golden retriever, and Baby, our black Labrador mix; we tried dressing them as Mr. and Mrs. Claus, but they were not too happy about it and the costumes were a bit tight. However, all the dogs got to wear collars with jingle bells on them to keep them in the spirit of Christmas; it was kind of funny to hear the bells jingling when the dogs were running as a pack.

By midmonth, we had set aside all thoughts of business plans, olive oil and the like; we wanted to enjoy ourselves during the holidays. We held one of our first themed *comidas*, a Korean barbecue cooked over two single-burner stoves with convex metal grills, which were placed at the center of the table; we offered marinated chicken, pork, beef and shrimp, accompanied by rice and various small dishes of vegetables such as garlic, scallions, carrots, peppers, jalapeños and bean sprouts, as well as bowls of romaine lettuce leaves. Participants would select the meat they wanted to cook, and once it was done to their taste they would take lettuce leaves and make lettuce rolls for themselves; we also served hot saké, which helped create a very festive and talkative atmosphere.

On December 17, one year and six days after my stent had been put in, I underwent a thorough battery of tests at the state-of-the-art Heart Center Institute in Querétaro, where my Mexican cardiologist practiced in addition to the hospital in SMA; everything was found to be fine. During the return trip, we stopped at the Antea LifeStyle Center in Querétaro, supposedly the largest shopping mall in Latin America at the time. I was in heaven; inside the mall, I felt like I was back in the United States. We had time to visit only one of the anchor stores, which was called *Palacio de Hierro* (The Iron Palace), before heading to the gourmet shop on the top floor, where we proceeded to the olive-oil section.

As we were purchasing some truffle oil, we noticed a counter displaying delicacies such as caviar and truffles; we then bought several small jars of black truffle mushrooms because we wanted to experiment with making our own black truffle oil. Walking around in the mall, we saw many stores with the same global brands as those in the United States. Since I had been fasting for my tests, we also went to the food court and treated ourselves to our first Burger King meal in Mexico.

At the same time, some of our friends were really showing interest in our project. During the Korean barbecue, I had remarked that there are a lot of fine products in Mexico for which the country is not well known, then related an incident during a long road trip in Mexico back in 2007: I had stopped at a coffee shop in Pátzcuaro and had an incredibly good cup of coffee; I had asked what country it was from and been told that it was Mexican coffee from Veracruz, which had surprised me because I had never heard of Mexican coffee. One of my new friends had replied that he had a small coffee plantation in Veracruz and that he would like to send me some green coffee beans to see what we could do with them; just before the Christmas holidays, we received a large burlap sack of coffee beans from Veracruz weighing one hundred kilograms (two hundred twenty pounds)!

I immediately bought several books online about roasting coffee. Previously, I had always thought that Italian roast was related to Italian coffee and French roast to French coffee, but our books indicated that roasting coffee beans crack like popcorn and that if one stops roasting the coffee after the first crack, it is referred to as Italian roast, whereas if the roasting ends after the second crack, it is called French roast.

After reading the books, we began experimenting. For our first coffee-roasting attempt, we placed a cast-iron skillet on one of the stovetop burners, and then put about half a pound of the green coffee beans into the skillet; as we gently stirred the beans inside the hot pan, they began to slowly change color and give off a wonderful aroma. We stopped the roasting process after the second crack in order to get our French roast. Even though it was three o'clock in the afternoon and we normally have coffee early in the morning, we could hardly wait to have the first cup of our own home-roasted coffee; after allowing the beans to cool for about ninety minutes, we ground them for use in our coffeemaker. Since the color and aroma of the coffee were exquisite, we were surprised when we poured our first cup only to discover that it tasted horrible; we threw out the coffee that we had brewed and saved the rest of the roasted coffee beans in a jar.

When two more attempts during the next several days produced similar results, we were almost ready to give up; the brewed coffee had a peculiar taste like burnt wood. I kept researching and finally discovered that our green coffee beans still had husks, so we pulled out our trusty KitchenAid mixer, put two or three handfuls of green coffee beans into the mixing bowl and turned on the mixer at the highest setting; sure enough, the husks started coming off. We then roasted the cleaned green coffee beans in the cast-iron pan to our usual French roast level; this time, the brewed coffee was not that great but was acceptable for a first try. Over the subsequent two or three months, we perfected the roasting process and taught María and Rosa how to do it; they are now experts who roast coffee better than we ever did.

By December 24, our little store had begun to take shape. We hung pictures on the walls, two cabinets had been completed and Transito started working on making a round table four feet in diameter. The talavera jugs were prominently displayed on the top shelf over the cabinets, and we also put several bottles of olive oil on display, as well as some of the preserves that Susan had made in the last twenty-four months.

For some reason, yellow lemons are not readily available in the stores in SMA; we had planted yellow-lemon trees several years ago, and this year the fruit began to ripen in late fall. Susan started to put wedges of the lemons in heavy-salt brine; when I asked her what she was doing, she replied that she was preserving the lemons in a Moroccan style. Unbeknownst to her, I immediately logged into Amazon.com and ordered her surprise Christmas present; I kept it hidden for most of the month, and on Christmas morning I gave her the gift to open. When she saw that it was a very expensive French tagine, she was elated; I knew that since she is a very good and adventurous cook, she would soon be trying new recipes that utilize her Moroccan lemons.

On Christmas Day, we invited a group of friends to *comida*; some of them had young children, and it was fun to celebrate the holidays with children around the house. Susan, knowing the children would be coming, had bought toys for them, but one of the kids was more interested in taking apart our flowers and other plants; however, the child quickly abandoned this activity when he realized that he could stomp around in the outdoor water fountain. His father soon joined him, and they both needed towels afterward.

To us, no holiday season is complete without a trip to Mi Casa at El Instituto; a small restaurant with an incredible view of the *parroquia* (parish) in SMA that has consistently good and very inexpensive food, it is also where Gil Gutierrez and his group of musicians play in the evening. There we had a wonderful dinner and were joined by Gil's son and daughter, both of whom were visiting during the holidays.

Having spent a delightful holiday season with our friends, we turned down all the invitations to join them on New Year's Eve. This is one of the few nights when our staff can celebrate a full holiday as a family, since Susan and I reserve December 31 to be alone together for a wonderful evening during which we enjoy champagne and a specially prepared meal; we also download our pictures for the entire year into our computer and play a continuous slideshow of them on our big-screen TV until either it is time for the Times Square Ball to drop or we fall asleep, whichever comes first.

2014 was a wonderful year that began full of trepidation about health concerns and ended with a celebration of the beginning of a new lifestyle.

Zandunga! January 2015

Gil and Rebecca invited us to a New Year's Day party celebrating the completion of his country venue; arriving at the venue, we saw that he had invited nearly eighty friends, most of whom we knew. For once, Gil was not the main musical attraction; he had engaged a mariachi group with ten musicians to provide the entertainment. Quite a bit of mezcal and tequila was consumed, and we were truly happy for Gil and Rebecca. In a private discussion with Gil, he told us that by the end of the month he expected to be performing concerts every Sunday and that he would be charging an admission fee; he then asked us whether we would be willing to conduct tastings of our olive oil at his venue on each Sunday, and we eagerly accepted the offer, since it presented an exciting opportunity.

Our strategy was simple: we would present our olive oil at tastings during Gil's concerts, and when people inquired about where to buy it, we would tell them that they could find it in our farm store. Since we expected that people would start coming to our store, we immediately began stocking the store with more of our products; at the time, our store had only two cabinets, a round table, a few bottles of olive oil and a lot of preserves that Susan had made in the last two years.

Our most immediate obstacle in putting products on the shelf was the label; the ones we had printed at

Office Depot were nearly impossible to separate from their protective paper layer, so we decided to scrap those labels, returning to Office Depot to purchase large printable adhesive labels. We then found a website that allowed us to design our logo specifically for the new labels.

Since we were still seeking the right bottles for our olive oil, we drove to our favorite talavera manufacturer in the nearby town of Dolores Hidalgo, bringing one of our two-hundred-fifty-milliliter bottles and the tagine that I had given Susan for Christmas. We worked with the fabricator to design some very attractive cream-colored talavera oil bottles that were all decorated with an image of an olive-laden branch; we then ordered one hundred of these bottles, as well as reusable molds and ten monochromatic copies of the tagine in the five basic colors offered, two for each color.

On the way back from Dolores Hidalgo, we made two stops. At the first stop, we purchased a crescent-moon-shaped piece of mesquite wood about four inches thick and seven feet wide that we thought would make a perfect countertop for a tasting bar. The second stop was at a local ranch that was selling beans at the ridiculously low price of ten cents per pound; we purchased two very large sacks of nearly one hundred pounds of pink beans each. I had a plan for those beans, but I did not tell Susan about it at the time; I hoped to offer them as part of a simple Mexican lunch we would provide for people coming to buy our olive oil in the not-too-distant future.

When we returned home with the cargo, I asked Transito to build a metal base for the countertop and the sacks of beans were placed in one corner of the store.

On January 17, Gil performed his first paid concert at the venue that he and Rebecca had named Zandunga, a word denoting a type of waltz in Gil's home state of Oaxaca; however, we were not yet ready to present our olive oil. Over the course of the following week, we proceeded to finalize our in-store offerings.

Transito and Juan were building the cabinets incredibly fast. By January 19, they had constructed a full complement of furniture, which included three cabinets, a round table and the mesquite-wood tasting counter; our glazier had fitted a glass finish to the contour of the mesquite as well. In a local artisan's shop, Susan found handmade greenish oxidized-brass knobs, which were then mounted onto the cabinet doors; the wooden cabinets themselves were painted with clear polyurethane. Below the shelf holding the colorful talavera *garrafóns*, we placed boxes of the empty bottles that would be filled with the olive oils the customers selected. The white walls and linen-like ceiling cover contrasted nicely with the red tiled floor. For a country establishment, the overall look was rather classy.

We purchased sixteen-ounce jars with lids, which we planned to fill with our cured olives. The olives that we had begun curing in September 2014 were not yet ready for consumption, but our olives from the previous year were excellent; we decided to pack them in the jars with mild red-wine-vinegar brine, then place the jarred olives on top of the cabinets.

Some of the *garrafóns* were filled with our "Arbequina" extra-virgin olive oil, others with our rosemary-, garlic-, basil- and lemon-infused oils; in the process, the *garrafóns* were labeled according to the oils they contained. The printed labels for these oils were also applied to the empty bottles, and under each *garrafón* we placed a case of the corresponding empty labeled bottles.

We also designed and printed our own business cards; on one side of each card was the telephone number we had allocated to the business, on the other a small map showing how to reach our place. At last, we were ready for our tastings at Zandunga.

The concerts at Zandunga were very informal; the setting was unlike theaters or restaurants. Since the customers had already purchased their tickets in town during the week, they each surrendered a ticket at the bar and received a free drink. As the band played, people were free to wander around the property, dancing or sitting wherever they pleased or getting something to eat at the food stations.

During the Saturday prior to the next concert, we transported our crescent-moon-shaped tasting bar to the venue, and Susan bought five loaves of very good French bread from one of the better-known high-quality bakeries in town. On January 24, we conducted our first formal tasting. We kept it simple: our glass-finished tasting counter was positioned in a corner with a clear side view of the room where the band played; Susan wore a green-striped shirt, I wore a white shirt with a black leather vest and we both wore jeans. Susan and I were a bit nervous at first, but shortly we were in our Madison Avenue presentation mode and began developing an educational style. Behind the counter, we had several olive oils in labeled two-hundred-fifty-milliliter bottles that had been fitted with plastic pourers, and Susan had brought a wooden cutting-board and a knife for slicing thin pieces of the French bread to serve with paper plates and napkins; when people approached to ask what we were offering, we would present our olive oil for tasting on the slices of bread. The tasting was an all-around success: everyone loved our olive oil, and many people were surprised that it came from olives grown and pressed in San Miguel de Allende; they all seemed enthusiastic and interested in visiting our farm to purchase the oil.

That night, we went home extremely excited, anticipating that many people would visit our little country store. Boy, were we in for a surprise! During the entire week, we did not have a single customer and the business phone never rang. We soon realized that we would be in this for the long haul, but we were

undeterred; by the following Sunday, we had
sharpened the delivery of our presentation until we
were ready to do it all again.

Selling Our Product: February 2015

Roughly four years earlier, Transito and his family had operated a small produce stand at their house in town; every Saturday, the family would go to Celaya and visit the Central de Abastos, a huge wholesale market occupying approximately five city blocks where storeowners can purchase products and produce in bulk. Susan and I wanted to see what this place is like, so Transito drove us in his truck to get bottles in Irapuato during the first week of February, stopping in Celaya along the way. At the market, we bought pineapples and mangoes to experiment with making vinegar from them. Afterward, we proceeded to Irapuato, where we purchased a larger quantity of bottles and jars because we expected sales to increase over the next several months.

By mid-February, Zandunga was gaining notoriety and drawing an average of almost one hundred patrons every Sunday; we observed that there were very few regulars, resulting in a different crowd each week. The clientele kept increasing, so Gil and Rebecca had expanded the venue's capacity by adding shade cover to a large section contiguous to the building where the band played. Everything was beginning to function efficiently; the entrance fee had been set at four hundred pesos, and in addition to attending a concert the customers received a free drink and all the tacos and quesadillas they could eat. In the area under the shade cloth, two new menu items were introduced: chicken wings barbecued on a gas grill and *tacos al pastor*, which are tacos made with meat cooked on a gyros-grilling machine; these were an instant hit, and a long line of people patiently waited for their servings. Since our bar had been relocated there, the traffic caused by the demand for wings and tacos boosted the number of people tasting our olive oil.

Gil and Rebecca were aware that we were still plugging away at our business plan but not attracting any visitors to the store at our farm; upon opening the new shaded area, they asked us whether we wanted to sell our olive oil at Zandunga, and we accepted the generous offer. We then jarred Susan's cured olives in a mixture of oil and fine herbs so we could offer them for sale as well and purchased clear plastic bags that the customers would use to carry home the merchandise.

On the following Sunday, we brought one of our cabinets as well as our crescent-moon-shaped tasting bar; we also brought our *garrafóns*, but they were only for display purposes, since we felt that filling bottles would be too time consuming. Our entire product line was offered in bottles or jars, including cases of each type of bottled olive oil, and we conducted tastings of both olives and oils. We based our prices on those at the olive-oil store in town, which were substantially higher than what the local supermarkets charged. Judging by the typical reactions to our tastings, we expected that we would need more staff, so Rosa and Transito joined us; Rosa was responsible for ringing up customers, keeping a record of our sales and slicing the bread, while Transito bagged the customers' purchases. My presentations to potential customers changed dramatically, shifting more toward educating people about olives and their oil; utilizing the knowledge I had gained from all my reading, I was talking about antioxidants and polyphenols, as well as the story of how our olive oil came to be—even my cholesterol reduction!

Our sales results were outstanding; very quickly, we began making an average of between two thousand and four thousand pesos on each Sunday, which at the time was equivalent to between one hundred fifty and three hundred dollars. Considering the state of the local economy, it was a good start that exceeded our projections. The reception of our products was also excellent; we estimated that more than ninety percent of the people who tasted our products bought them.

Our farm continued to be a beehive of activity. When our peach and olive trees began to bloom, I became very concerned about the weather because we were susceptible to light freezes in February and even early March. Having owned a farm in Florida, we were familiar with this danger; however, in Florida we had had an alarm system that would wake us up if the temperature started getting close to freezing, in which case we would rev up the diesel engines that had operated the pumps for our irrigation system and make it rain on our thirty acres. The water would release some heat first, thus preventing the trees from freezing until sunrise, but since we had no such protection in Mexico, we had to accept whatever nature threw at us.

We purchased a set of used teak furniture from one of our friends, which we decided to put on the roof terrace where a custom-made rectangular awning provided some shade. However, the shaded area was too small for the furniture, so I asked Transito to build us a bigger shelter using locally available bamboo-like reeds known as carrizos. Our roof terrace, approximately thirty feet long and wide, was constructed to be the floor of a second story; over the years, I had deliberated about what to do with the space, as it had incredible three-hundred-sixty-degree views from the top of our house. Therefore, Transito was to build a temporary shelter to fit over our teak furniture so I could make sure that we would utilize this space; if it proved effective, then we would erect a more permanent structure. When it was completed, we found that the shady area under the carrizo combined with the teak furniture, which we had restored to its natural finish, to add a new dimension on our property; it quickly became one of our favorite entertainment venues and was incorporated into our plan as a dining area created a little bit ahead of schedule.

Pablo and Denise invited us to go with them to a Korean restaurant in Querétaro, where we met with them and had a great dinner; afterward, they introduced us to a store that sold Korean and other Asian products. The clerks were Mexican, but they clearly understood the imported products they were offering; I had a short discussion with them as Susan was buying imports such as sauces and pastes. Apparently, it was a brand-new store that the owners had modeled on their first store in Monterrey; their clientele consisted of expatriate Korean employees of various companies that manufactured electronic devices in the vicinity. We had brought from Florida to Mexico a small single-burner stovetop fueled by a can of gas that we had been unable to find in SMA; I was very happy to see that this store carried not only the fuel cans but also the stoves, since our plan involved using them. I purchased eight fuel cans, two additional single-burner stoves and four little aluminum pots with ear-like handles on their sides; when I rejoined Susan, she knew immediately what I was planning, so that while I was picking up four bottles of saké, she proceeded to collect some vegetables that would complement one of my favorite dishes.

Shabu shabu is a Japanese hotpot dish in which the ingredients are brought raw to a pot sitting on a burner in the center of the table; the pot contains hot water and sometimes a piece of seaweed, and the raw ingredients are usually thinly sliced beef or pork accompanied by cabbage, onions and any other vegetable that cooks quickly in boiling water. Once the water is boiling and the raw food is delivered, one selects the desired food and puts it in the boiling water; when the food is cooked, one takes it out of the water and dips it into one of two sauces before eating it. I like this particular style of cooking and dining because it creates a conversational atmosphere, since the meal lasts for a couple hours.

Arriving home from our trip to Querétaro, we knew that we had all the necessary ingredients except the meat, so we went to our local Soriana supermarket at the Luciérnaga Mall; after a long conversation with the butcher, we were able to obtain thinly sliced raw beef. On the following day, Susan and I enjoyed our first shabu shabu meal at our house in Mexico; among the fresh vegetables was our home-grown bok choy. We added this type of meal to our *comida* repertoire and in subsequent months introduced quite a few people to shabu shabu.

As a result of our successful presentations at Zandunga, we were invited to an opera performed at one of the local wineries, where our presentation was met with equal success. During this period, all the compliments we were receiving from total strangers were going to my head, so that when a couple acquaintances became very animated about investing in our business, without thinking I quickly put together a proposal to expand our business to various towns across Mexico; this was a very stupid move, as our inventory volume was minuscule compared to the needs of such an enterprise. The expansion plans accelerated when a deposit was put down for a store location within SMA city limits; I was excited at the moment, as were the acquaintances I had partnered with. However, on the next day I woke up completely rational and called off the plans for a store in town; fortunately, we were able to recoup the deposit funds. Returning to my senses, I resolved to stick to the plan that Susan and I had meticulously developed.

Pablo and Denise again invited us to Querétaro, but this time Pablo was giving a presentation to a group of wine enthusiasts and invited us to conduct a tasting of our products and sell them at the event. It was our first event at which we did not have the blanket of security that our friends in SMA provided, so Susan and I were a bit nervous when we arrived; however, as seasoned executives who had presented in some of the most hostile environments on Madison Avenue, we quickly regained our composure. Our products were a hit once more, and this time the sales exceeded our expectations; on the way home, we were talking so excitedly about our accomplishment that we missed our exit to SMA and wound up driving for thirty minutes through one of Querétaro's industrial parks.

Living in the countryside has its surprises; on one particular night, we were driving up our road when less than five hundred feet from our front entrance, we saw a very large bobcat. At the time, I paid no attention to this sighting; however, over the next several days the bobcat visited our poultry pens and killed three turkeys, so we took precautionary measures by completely covering the pens with chicken wire.

The chickens and turkeys were no longer pets but part of our business plan for their aesthetic value as well as their eggs; in fact, we included all our animals in our business plan, taking every aspect into account. Their current and future appearances were planned for, so that we started shearing the sheep and grooming the horses more often. We also began cleaning the pens and corrals daily and implemented a management system for manure composting—we even envisioned organically controlling flies!

Our farm was no longer a hobby; the more successes we scored, the more we invested in our plan. This was a progressive enterprise with key milestones that had to be met, and we were exceeding them!

We Are Blessed! My Christ: March 2015

March was a month full of local culinary experiences; since we wanted to offer an eatery, we needed to see, taste and price the fare provided by our nearest competitors. I have always been extremely cautious about where and what I eat; over my professional career of nearly fifty years that involved a lot of travel, the victuals in almost every country I visited made me ill at one time or another, and I am especially wary of food in Mexico. Given this, one may be just as surprised by the following story as I was.

Early in the month, Susan and I decided to try the local *barbacoa* place that Transito had mentioned, so we drove down our dirt road, made a left turn at the blacktop and pulled into the parking lot in front of the diner after traveling a distance of about three hundred feet. The restaurant is more like a large hall approximately forty feet wide and sixty feet long, and the chairs and tables are of the plastic type found in almost all roadside eateries in our area.

On the far left corner is a counter where customers place their orders; we each ordered four tacos and a consommé for a cost of four dollars and fifty cents, then sat at a small table. After the attendant had brought our meal, we used the typical hot sauces, lime, cilantro and onion to garnish our tacos, and when we each took a bite, chewing slowly to taste it before swallowing,

Transito's claim proved to be true—these tacos were indeed superior to the ones I had enjoyed en route to Hidalgo. Having finished our tacos, next we garnished the consommé, which was also much better than that offered by the eatery where I had previously dined; this incredibly delicious consommé contained garbanzos, squash and onions. We loved the food, the setting, the new way to have breakfast and particularly how close the place is to our house—we can order Mexican takeout there.

La Casita, a very small eatery with seating for fourteen people, is situated about twenty feet away from the heavily traveled road that serves as the main entry into SMA from Mexico City or Querétaro; it offers an all-you-can-eat buffet for three dollars and fifty cents per person, including a bottle of water or a soft drink. The buffet is always the same; displayed on a steam table are trays of basic red rice, scrambled eggs with beans in a red sauce, pork rind in another red sauce, *nopales* (cactus pads) with peppers, *chorizo* (hot sausage) in sauce, as well as beef and potatoes in sauce. These sauce dishes are known as *guisados* (stews). I love the food at La Casita, but unfortunately I cannot go there often because I have a tendency to overeat at the place and so would gain too much weight.

We can reach the center of town in several ways, which we choose based on our destination; one of our least-used routes is through a section called the Atascadero, a very rough cobblestoned road that at times is so narrow that only one car can fit through. At the beginning of the road's descent, we pass the entrance to the Atascadero Hotel; on a day when we were out exploring, Susan and I decided to stop by and ask whether they have a restaurant. After we had been directed through the hotel and various courtyards, we came to a very large dining room that we estimated would easily seat one hundred fifty people; the wall opposite its entry is made of wooden windows that let the light in through the tall trees outside, creating an atmosphere similar to that of a large country inn in the northern regions of the United States.

We sat at a table near one of the windows and ordered margaritas and guacamole; though it was twelve thirty in the afternoon, we were the only people in the restaurant besides the attentive staff. Having assumed that the place would fill up as traditional lunchtime approached, usually at around two o'clock, we were surprised to see only one other couple come in before we left. Our lunch was acceptable; we both had *arrachera* with grilled vegetables. As we walked out of the restaurant, we noticed that there is an outdoor seating area and made a mental note to return.

Not a week had passed before we were sitting outside the restaurant, enjoying our drinks, burgers and fries in the warm March sunshine. This place has become like our private Shangri-La, where we go for discussions and quiet moments, since there are seldom many people. The hotel, which has over one hundred rooms, is extremely busy on weekends and hosts a lot of weddings, but scales down its staff when tourism dwindles; however, it always keeps the restaurant open to ensure that all systems are operational.

Susan developed a recipe for tapenade, a paste made of ground olives and capers that contains dried red tomatoes, garlic and other spices, as well as a little bit of anchovy fillet. At our tastings, we gave potential customers a small piece of French bread with tapenade spread on it; we also sold the paste in a nine-ounce jar with a metal lid, and it quickly became one of our most popular products. We do not use any preservatives, and we make the tapenade every week.

Our vinegars were beginning to complete their fermentation process; Susan measured their acidity levels and found them to be adequate. We researched and implemented a pasteurization procedure to terminate the fermentation, then filled two-hundred-fifty-milliliter bottles with the two vinegars that were ready to be sold, which had been made with apples and pomegranates picked from our trees.

A very good Mexican-American singer well known in Chicago had arranged to sing with Gil during a trip to SMA. Gil instinctively knew that she would be a big draw and that Zandunga lacked the capacity to accommodate the expected crowd, so he called our friends at Dos Buhos Winery and rented the large hall. He held a concert for approximately three hundred people, and we set up the tasting counter and other equipment for our shop in one corner of the hall; once again, more people were introduced to our olive oil.

During our entire relationship of over fifteen years, Transito has shown himself to be a devout Catholic. When Susan had completed the remodel of our home back in 2001, Transito had brought a priest, who had blessed all the buildings and animals on our property; to this day, he frequently comments about how blessed our property is.

I was brought up in a Catholic family; my parents were devout Catholics to the day they died, as are my brother and sister, which I guess makes me the black sheep of the family. Nevertheless, I too received a religious education, graduating with the required minor in theology from a Jesuit university in the eastern US. Although I do not attend church unless there is a wedding or death in the family, I am a believer; I have read the Bible cover to cover and still say my prayers every night.

Throughout the years, many things have happened on our property that makes me believe, as Transito does, that our property is indeed blessed. For some reason, crops that are not expected to grow well in our area flourish on our property, and animals thrive and proliferate there. The property has a tranquil ambience that one feels from the moment one enters through the front gates, which one does not experience anywhere else. We have lots of birds of many varieties on our property, and one can watch them frolic in any of our fountains for hours. Our seven dogs, two of which are fairly ferocious-looking German shepherds, threaten to tear visitors apart as soon as they see them on our property, but once the dogs realize that the visitors are our friends, they become very tame, lovable pets.

In 2015, Easter Sunday fell on April 5. Since the previous Sunday had been Palm Sunday, Transito had placed palm leaves in various locations throughout our houses and property, as is our custom. We have a series of themed gardens: a maze, a traditional English herb garden, a pine-tree garden, a citrus-fruit garden, an orchard and what we call the beach garden, a quadrangle approximately fifty feet long and wide that has only sand as the groundcover and is planted with queen palms, date palms and palmettos. Palm trees can be either self-cleaning or not self-cleaning; the fronds of self-cleaning palms fall cleanly off the trunk when they dry, whereas those of palms that are not self-cleaning hang from the trunk when untrimmed, giving it the appearance of wearing a skirt below its green crown. Palmettos are not self-cleaning, and we have one that is approximately sixty feet high.

To get to the point, on March 31, 2015, the Tuesday following Palm Sunday, I was sitting in our den and looking out the window at the tops of the palm trees; their gentle swaying motion in the wind can be hypnotic. Suddenly, my eyes were diverted to the skirt on the tall palmetto; I stared in disbelief for quite a few minutes, then grabbed my iPhone, turned on the camera and took several pictures. When I saw the pictures, I knew that my eyes were not deceiving me—the fronds on the tree formed a large profile of

Christ. The hairline, forehead, eyes, nose, mouth, mustache and beard were all clearly visible.

Wondering whether it was merely my imagination or I was going nuts, I kept it to myself for a day until finally I told Susan and then Transito; they both saw the outlines of the face, but were unmoved by it, whereas I was awed. When I sent the picture to my brother and sister, they also did not have the intense reaction to it that I was feeling. I even showed it to a couple of visitors only to get the same blasé response, at which point I stopped talking to people about it; however, for most of the year I carried my Christ with me, and just knowing he was there consoled me.

As I recount our developing story, I refer to my digital folder of nearly three thousand pictures for the period covered by this book, trying to select the highlights that distinguish each month from all the others; a lot of the activity on a farm (or any business, for that matter) is repetitive and keeps the entire staff busy. Frankly, the appearance of my Christ made March a very special month; it occurred not only on the last day of the month but also during Holy Week—need I say more?

More Staff, More Products: April 2015

Our first April event at Zandunga took place on Easter Sunday. Jamie, an artist who was one of our new friends, was invited by Gil to show and sell his paintings during the event; the only one that caught my eye happened to be on the wall facing our tasting counter. I kept staring at that painting of a burro (small donkey) for quite a while, and the donkey stared back; I finally gave in to the donkey, and we purchased the painting. For some reason, I felt that this painting would be an interesting decoration for our store; we spent more money on it than we had made on the olive oil we had sold to date, but Susan and I kept separate budgets and everything else was going according to plan.

By this time, we believed that we had the Sunday events under control and so we began focusing more on our overall plan and our growing farm. For the last fifteen years, we had funded ourselves totally from monies earned outside of Mexico, and we projected that our enterprise would generate profits in Mexico; thus, we seriously started to look for legal and tax professionals who would provide us with the appropriate advice. One of our recent acquaintances suggested a firm located in San Luis Potosí, and we scheduled an appointment there for ten o'clock in the morning on Wednesday, April 8.

After departing from our house at midday on April 7, we checked into a very unique hotel; its exterior façade and courtyard were impressive. It was being converted to a Hilton and therefore undergoing a major renovation, but our room was in a completed section.

Susan had researched the available attractions, as she does every time we travel to an unfamiliar city; soon after checking in, we took a taxi to the historic center of town, where we strolled around the Central District, visiting various churches and admiring the colonial architecture of assorted government buildings. Our main destination, however, was the National Mask Museum; Susan has always been interested in masks and has a small collection at our home. This particular museum contains a very large collection of pre-Hispanic to present-day Mexican masks for dances and rituals. I do not enjoy museums much, so after walking around the museum for about an hour, I found a comfortable chair to sit in while waiting for Susan. Returning to our hotel at around seven o'clock at night, we went to its restaurant and relished our meal in the outdoor courtyard under the stars.

On the next day, our meeting with a lawyer/accountant lasted approximately one hour, then Susan and I returned to our hotel and checked out. During the two-hour ride back to our home, we came to the conclusion that we would work with this professional only if we had no other option; we preferred to find someone from our local area or at least closer to us.

Upon our return home, Transito expressed concern that Ani, our full-breed Dorper ewe, did not appear to be getting pregnant. We contacted our vet and had our first experience with modern veterinary technology at the farm; our vet brought a small machine that he used to give Ani a sonogram. He found everything to be normal, and some months later Ani would indeed give birth.

During the past several years, Gil had been touring the northeastern US with a very good violinist; together they traveled to various venues and performed concerts for about a month. This year was no different except that Gil planned to do some additional construction on his venue as soon as he returned; the last event at Zandunga before it closed until the beginning of July was held on April 19.

On the following day, we collected our tasting bar and cabinet. As we were returning to the house, Transito and I passed a place selling rustic farm antiques; there we spotted another piece of mesquite wood that could serve as a countertop. We came home, unloaded our cargo and headed back to check out the mesquite; we liked what we saw, so I purchased three potential countertops. I loved the look and feel of our mesquite tasting counter, and we already needed one for Zandunga and one for the store; therefore, to allow for expansion we bought more mesquite than necessary.

As our business and product development expanded, it became evident that some things were not getting completely done by the staff; our greenhouse was looking a little ragged, and the cottage needed a thorough cleaning since we expected to rent it soon. I had no doubt that María and Rosa would eventually catch up with the work, but we were already planning additional products that would use the fruit on the blossoming trees and bushes; therefore, we asked Juana, Transito's daughter-in-law, and Maribel, his second-oldest daughter, whether they would like to come bring their children (Juana had two daughters who were four and five years old, and Maribel had a six-month-old baby girl and a four-year-old daughter) from Transito's house in town and work for us during afternoons when the girls are at school.

They accepted our offer, and in effect we added the equivalent of one staff member. Juana and Maribel were put in charge of maintaining the greenhouse and cottage, keeping the store organized and clean, the entire vinegar-making process and bottling the olive oil and vinegars. Having lots of children around made our place even happier.

Susan and I began experimenting with making jellies, which is not as easy as simply following recipes; one can go through a lot of work only to end up with a liquid substance that does not gel. Once we had the system fairly well established, we delegated it to María, Rosa, Maribel and Juana; under their charge, the jelly making would follow the fruit harvest all the way into late September.

Our big fifty-seven-inch-wide flat-screen TV began shutting itself off in the middle of a program; we talked to several technicians, but none were able to fix it. I finally gave up on the television, bought a new one and put the faulty one in the store. Next I spent most of the week putting together a slideshow about the history of olive oil, which had background music and seventy-eight slides; after putting it on a memory stick that I then plugged into the back of the defective television, I successfully played this slideshow on the television in the store. This project would have a future role in our store, but I was finished with it for the moment.

We were getting a lot of notoriety from our tasting events; in early April, we received a visit from the management team of a local organic restaurant and store, as well as a country farm that supplies the restaurant, sells its products in various local organic markets and provides schooling and training for rural folks. The team gave us a brief explanation of a project that entailed organic egg production; they planned to plant olive trees under which the chickens would range free, and we agreed to provide them with guidance on selecting the trees. They also asked us whether we would be willing to conduct tastings of our olive oil and sell it in their store, as well as at an upcoming street fair that would be held in town near their restaurant. By month's end, we were participating in our first street fair in SMA, and Susan had spent several days offering tastings and selling our oil on their premises; these efforts were not very successful, but they did give us insight on a different type of customer from the ones at Zandunga.

Since we had owned and operated a plant and tree nursery in Florida, one could say that plant and tree propagation is in our blood; we really enjoy it. Knowing that in Mexico we did not have the appropriate equipment for the initial stages of propagation, we opted to acquire olive seedlings ready for their first stage of potting; properly caring for these very young saplings would result in trees ready for planting at the time of our projected expansion. Transito took charge of the nursery operation and also started to experiment with making our own cuttings to begin the process of propagation.

Extending Horizon~~I Am out of Here~~: May 2015

The period from the end of April to the beginning of
May is when temperatures rise in SMA, climbing into
the nineties during the daytime. This weather
continues until the rains start, which normally occurs
around mid- to late June, though there are no
guarantees; surprises can happen due to an early rain
in May or a late one sometime in July. Frankly, most
people get cranky because of the dust and the heat, and
many leave on vacation if they do not have school-age
children; as a result, the tourists are practically
nonexistent and the town is not very busy.

We were unprepared for the accumulating warmth
inside our store, which can deteriorate olive oil rapidly;
when the indoor temperature began rising above
seventy, we needed to take action. The most immediate
step was putting shade-polarizing screens on all the
glass; we had brought quite a bit of this material from
Florida, so we used a big roll of it after carrying it out of
our storage room. Juan already knew how to apply the
film on the glass; before the afternoon was over, the
windows and doors were properly shaded to reduce
the amount of sunlight in the store. Although this
measure was a good start, it did not have a major effect
on the heat buildup.

Our main difficulty was the sheet-metal roof; as the
metal warmed in the sun, it radiated heat into the store.

Transito and I discussed various ways to correct the problem, including tearing down all the sheet metal and laying a concrete roof; while this method would be ideal, it would also be time consuming and expensive. We decided that the best solution was to lay tejas on top of the roof, which are the porous red clay roof tiles used in traditional California mission-style architecture.

First, however, we needed to support the central beam in the store's roof with a column; the tejas would be heavy, and their weight would increase when wet. After measuring the distance between the beam and the floor, we decided that a post six inches square would suffice; at the lumberyard, we were fortunate to find a round post six inches in diameter, the exact dimension we were looking for. When we returned to the store, we placed the post in the appropriate location, and the result was excellent; the post did not look like an afterthought but actually blended well with the store's décor.

We then purchased the tejas, and they were laid on top of the sheet metal, resulting in a very good-looking roof whose tiles matched those on our other buildings. The temperature in the store was drastically reduced, never rising higher than seventy degrees even on hot ninety-degree days. Nothing seemed to slow down our farm, and surprising new turns of events were about to happen.

Transito was busy constructing another tasting counter, this time with doors and cabinets underneath; it was smaller than the crescent-moon-shaped one, but we thought it would be fine for Zandunga. During this process, a young couple starting an organic marketplace came to our property; when they had toured the farm and tasted our products, they asked whether we would like to rent a space in their market where we would sell our products, to which we agreed after visiting their locale. The counter with built-in cabinets was then reallocated to the new location.

Since we neither wanted to wholesale our products to the couple nor let them handle our sales and money, we had agreed on a fixed-fee rental, planning to find someone else to manage our stand, inventory and funds. We did not have to search far; when we discussed it with Irma, Transito's eldest daughter with older children ranging in age from twelve to seventeen, she immediately accepted the job. The responsibility of training Irma fell upon Rosa, who had been selling at all of our events for the last two months.

Right from the start, we did not expect a large volume of sales at the stand; rather, we projected that we would recoup the costs of the merchandise, Irma's salary and the rental fee, thus breaking even. Instead, our main objectives for this enterprise were gaining retail experience, seeing how well our products sell, testing new products and most of all getting our name out—at Zandunga, more and more people asked where they could purchase our products, but none of them ever came to our farm store, so we were happy that we could provide a closer address situated on the road around the perimeter of the town. As our "town" location evolved, it slowly became more professional; we graduated from clear plastic grocery bags to nicer yellow-green ones with handles, removed the map to our farm from the back of our business card, having finally accepted that no customers would go there for a long while (the store's development had originally been planned for the end of the third year anyway), and experimented with using little plastic cups as well as the bread during presentations of our olive oil for tastings.

Our attention shifted to the horse pasture, where we were planting our young trees. In this area of a little more than three acres, we had used about an acre and a half for an organic garden and the grove; the organic vegetable garden was protected from the horses, but we were letting our horses graze among the newly planted trees. The horses did not seem interested in the olive trees, but rather would meander between them while eating the grass; however, we realized that the horses could trample them with ease, so we purchased over one thousand eight hundred feet of yellow nylon rope half an inch thick and cordoned off the perimeter of the grove, which allowed the horses to still graze on nearly two acres without jeopardizing the olive trees.

Pablo and Denise came to visit us with twelve of their friends, a wonderful group of people with whom we had bonded at the wine and olive oil tasting in

Querétaro where Pablo had given his presentation; they were our first official customers at the farm store, and it really boosted our morale to see people who actually knew about our products enthusiastically purchasing them at our farm store. They also provided us with insight, confirmed how special our little farm was becoming a destination point and even suggested that we conduct tours and charge people to enjoy our property; while this was indeed our ultimate goal, as realists we recognized that at the time we could not attract people to our property to sell our products, much less to have tours.

All the notoriety and excitement were having a positive effect on me; I was at the top of my game, taking well-calculated risks and feeling alive again, so that my negativity about Mexico began to disappear. Though my health was still imperfect, it was improving, and my relationship with Susan was stronger than ever as we truly enjoyed each other's company and that of the great group of friends we had developed. Moreover, it was springtime! Our jacarandas were displaying their purple splendor, our roses were in full bloom, we were making apricot jelly, our vinegars were almost ready, our orchids were blossoming and we were planting many more trees—life could not be better!

On Monday, May 19, we drove to the León airport to pick up my best friend, advisor and motivator- in-chief, otherwise known as Grace, who was then ninety-six years old. Her granddaughter McCleary and her friend Megan accompanied her. I have always welcomed her counsel, guidance and observations on all the crazy adventures that Susan and I have had, and I could not wait for her to experience what we were developing; her opinion mattered more to me than anyone else's.

We all spent our first night quietly at home, as we always do when we have visitors from New York or other lowlands; our house is almost seven thousand feet above sea level, and some people need a night's rest to adjust to the altitude. Over the next several days, we headed into town, did some sightseeing or relaxed at home. On Thursday night, we met with Gil and Rebecca at the Rosewood Hotel's rooftop cocktail bar, where we had a marvelous time sitting in the cool mountain air under the blankets provided, watching the sunset and enjoying the cocktails.

Grace was wonderfully inquisitive, guiding and counseling us on our business development. She has always pushed Susan and me to document and write about our experiences in order to share them with others; I do not believe Susan has ever taken this advice seriously, but about eighteen months earlier I had begun to write a book about the history of Luna Serena from 1999 to the present. I told Grace that I had started doing some writing but that I was too busy at the moment to conclude the book. One of the problems with having visitors from abroad, particularly family members, is that there is never enough time to spend together.

We invited Gil and Rebecca to join us for dinner on Friday night; Rebecca was not able to make it, but Gil did. As we were enjoying barbecued lamb chops with grilled vegetables and a salad, the dogs were barking unusually loudly and became so bothersome that we put them in the kitchen and closed the steel-bar door between the dining room and the kitchen. This door is part of our security system; when closed, it seals off the living room and bedrooms from the rest of the house, and the sealed section of the house also contains heavy window bars and double-locked doors for additional security. During the fifteen years we had owned our property, we had not had any incidents of burglaries or home invasion; a nine-foot-high wall approximately two thousand feet long lined the front of our driveway, and the rest of the property is fenced with barbed wire and containment wire to keep our animals in and others out. Our neighbors had all installed armed security because they had been robbed, whereas we had seven watchdogs.

As we were having dinner in our main dining room at around nine o'clock that night, two armed men wearing masks and hoods entered the room through the rear door; the door leading outside had apparently been left unlocked. One man was stocky, approximately five foot six and armed with a small-caliber revolver and a Taser; the other, slim and six feet tall with long, dark hair sticking out through the back of his hood, was armed with a chromed small-caliber pistol and a small-caliber revolver. Realizing what was happening, I started thinking fast; my first concern was for Grace, McCleary and Megan. Gil looked at me, thinking this was a joke, and I told him it was no joke.

They immediately closed the heavy wooden internal security doors, which are approximately two inches thick; it seemed that that these individuals were familiar with our house, since these sliding doors are not easily discernible to someone first visiting the house. At once, I asked them what they wanted, and when the tall one answered, I knew he was the leader; he said that they did not want to harm anyone and just wanted to take some things, to which I replied that we had nothing to take. He then said that they were looking for valuables, and I told him we had very little.

The short man walked to the chair where I had left my briefcase, which I took to my office every morning, and began rifling through the bag: I very quickly stood, ignoring the taller one as he yelled a command at me to sit down, then I went around the table, forcibly grabbed the bag from his hands, cursed at him, opened it and said, "What do you want with this? There's nothing here but my work papers." After zipping the bag closed, I threw it against his chest, adding, "If you want to take it, take it and get the hell out"; he picked up the bag, tossed it aside and moved on to the bedrooms. As the man passed our seven dogs behind the bars, they started growling and barking, particularly Tobi, our guard dog, and Hans and Greta, our two German shepherds.

I had protected the briefcase because it contained my passport in a travel kit, credit cards and a few thousand dollars I had foolishly kept there; realizing that I had outsmarted the little idiot, I began forming a plan to lure these two guys outside the house, leaving everyone else safe inside. Calmly walking back to my chair, I sat down and in a quavering voice told the leader, who remained in the room, that I had a very weak heart, that I had recently undergone a serious procedure and that the current stress was going to do me in. When he suggested I drink some water and calm down, assuring me that they would soon be gone, I knew that I could trick him too.

Laying my head on the table, I continued talking to distract the tall man as I fingered and slowly grasped the steak knife in front of me, but then I reasoned to myself, "What the hell are you going to do with a steak knife against two people, and the whole family watching?" Letting go of the knife, I instead sat back in my chair, started moaning and groaning and claimed that my

heart was failing and that I was in bad shape; Gil
chimed in to back me up, and Susan,
understanding what I was saying in Spanish, got
up and asked me in broken Spanish,
"Sweetheart, do you want me to go get your
heart pills?" I had to keep myself from laughing
not only because of her poor Spanish but also
because I had no heart pills; however, I realized
that she was just playing along. The dogs were
causing such a commotion that the leader
requested we quiet them down; Susan wanted
to know what he had said, so I translated. Her
calm answer was unforgettable, and when I told
the robber that she had suggested opening the
door, he looked a bit shaken; having seen that he
was easily manipulated, I decided to change the
game.

When Susan began rubbing my back, I became
concerned that she might entangle herself in my
plan, so I stood up and walked to the other side
of the table before telling the leader that I was
not feeling well and needed to go to the
bathroom. He ordered me to sit down, but I said,
"Stop me; I'm going" and proceeded to the
bathroom; he followed me. On the way, we
passed the little man, who was rifling through
drawers in the dark and wanted to know how to

turn the lights on; I told them both to go to hell and refused to switch on the lights. The tall man asked the short one why he had not taken the phone; the response was that the phone was only good for accessing the Internet. I stored this revealing exchange in the back of my mind, realizing that I could use the phone as soon as I got these guys out of our house; the plan was coming together.

I returned to the living room, followed by the tall man, who then said that he was going to lock us all into our sauna; I told him he was not going to lock me up anywhere. He led us to the bedroom next to the sauna; Gil, McCleary and Megan sat down in the sauna, but I would not cooperate. When he pointed a gun at me, I lied down on the bed and said, "Shoot me in my bed; I am going to die in thirty minutes, so it might as well be now." Susan also refused to enter, saying that she would allow neither herself nor her ninety-six-year-old mother to be imprisoned.

I lay in bed for a few seconds until I heard the rear heavy wooden door slide as the tall man went outside, at which point I ran out of the bedroom, leaving Susan and Grace behind, who were hugging each other in their chairs. As soon as I had reached the room where the telephone was, I called Transito; he had been in his apartment the whole time, just three hundred feet from our house. When I told him, "We have been robbed by two guys. They have run out the back; let's go get them," he calmly said that I should stay and secure the house; he would handle the rest and let me know when it was safe to come out. Transito immediately alerted the various neighbors' guards; shortly thereafter, we heard lots of gunfire all of a sudden and then quietness, which worried me—someone outside might have gotten hurt.

After about ten minutes, Transito came by and said the coast was clear; no one was hurt, and the thieves were nowhere to be found. He added that it was okay for us to call the police; when I did so, the response was almost immediate. In less than five minutes, a police team was at our gate; we chatted with them and they said that they would be on the lookout in case the robbers were still around.

Gil went home; after arriving there a few minutes later, he called us to say that we had nothing to fear, adding, "It's almost like the entire army is covering the road, heavily armed and even with night-vision goggles." The police had stopped him, asking him to come out of his car and provide identification.

In the end, the thieves got away with some spending money I had left on my dresser, inexpensive jewelry, my iPhone and my iPod, but no credit cards or documents; a piece of jewelry of great sentimental value to Susan was the only irreplaceable loss. The entire event took about forty-five minutes; I have given only a short summary. Gil and I had had some very intense discussions, the robbers had clearly been nervous and the situation had indeed been dangerous; however, everyone was safe, which was all that mattered.

Everyone wanted a drink, so we all went into the den. As we sat down, Grace was the first to speak, raising her glass to make a toast and chuckling as she said, "Here is to crossing another thing off my bucket list." She had broken the ice; we all started laughing about how amateurish the thieves had been, whom we nicknamed Dumb and Dumber. However, we still acknowledged that the robbers had been armed, on edge and therefore dangerous: we were all glad that no one, including Dumb and Dumber, had gotten hurt.

Megan was shattered by the entire incident; on Saturday, she was extremely upset and nervous, and plane reservations were made for her departure on Sunday. That particular Sunday was when Gil performed his first concert at Zandunga after his US tour, but Susan and I skipped the event and accompanied Megan to the airport. It is hard to say how everyone had felt on the night of the robbery because they had kept their feelings to themselves; however, I do know that for the next several days Susan and I felt violated and worried that the robbers would return, but were in no mood to talk about it.

Since Grace and McCleary were scheduled to depart from Mexico City, Susan took them there a few days early, and they checked into the Hotel Camino Real, visited museums and went sightseeing; however, on the morning when they would fly to New York, Grace did not feel well, so it was decided that Grace should not travel on that day. McCleary departed, and Grace returned to SMA with Susan.

After an appointment with Dr. Barrera and a discussion with Grace, the problem was diagnosed; Grace had forgotten one of her medications and had decided to skip it to avoid refilling it in Mexico. Dr. Barrera issued the medication, and plans were made for Grace's departure on the following Sunday; Susan accompanied her for a short visit to New York.

While Susan was away, I did a lot of thinking; I felt spiritually broken, and I hated living in Mexico more than ever before. Even though I loved the country and its people, our house and all that what we had accomplished, I wanted out because of the robbery. I kept recalling Susan's words as we went to bed on that night: "I am not going to let two punks run and ruin my life"; I knew that I needed to overcome my emotions just as Susan had, but it would not be as easy for me as it had been for her.

A Town Fair ~~Trying to Cope~~: June 2015

~~The robbery left us morose and extremely mad, but we still had to face reality and keep the farm and business going.~~

Next to the newly planted olive grove, we have two garden beds; one is fenced off to minimize animal incursions and planted with vegetables, alfalfa and beans. The second one had been planted during the previous June with corn, which had been harvested from September to October; after the corn harvest, it had lain fallow for a month, then had been planted with garlic. In 2015, we harvested approximately three hundred pounds of garlic. Fresh garlic is absolutely wonderful, particularly when just picked; its paper-thin skin is not dry but pulpy and succulent with an intense flavor that can only be experienced at a garlic farm during harvest season.

Our harvested garlic was left in Transito's workshop to dry for a few days in plastic baskets before being cleaned. The workshop, located near the chicken coops, the corrals and the sheep pens, was where a lot of construction and repair work was done; due to the proximity of the animals, it was also where the number of flies could be rather bothersome and at times intense. While visiting the workshop several days later, I observed that there were no flies in the shop; I pointed it out to Transito, and he too noticed it for the first time. We concluded that the garlic was keeping the flies away; after all, we used a homemade spray made from garlic, jalapeños and lemons as an organic pesticide for our crops. After putting the garlic in mesh bags holding about fifty pounds each, we placed two bags in the farm store and another by the back kitchen door; our utilization of the garlic as a fly repellent was very effective, and the bag by the kitchen door supplied garlic for culinary purposes as well. Infused garlic oil became one of our most popular products, and we were making at least a gallon every two weeks.

Beginning on the evening of Friday, June 12, we participated in the third annual Sabores San Miguel, a food festival held at Parque Juarez; all the top restaurants in town and several international chefs are invited to this three-day event, during which each participant operates a food stand, selling dishes that cost no more than twenty-five pesos. We were told that the event attracts an attendance of nearly ten thousand people, so we decided to stock up on our inventory for the expected sales, also ordering lots of French bread, paper plates and bowls for tastings; in addition, we planned to offer small bowls of olives as well as tapenade on slices of French bread for twenty-five pesos apiece.

The event started at six o'clock in the evening on Friday night. After tasting all our oils, our very first customer introduced himself as the owner of the shop that we considered our competition in town; he liked our olive oil and asked whether we would be willing to sell it in his store, which was quite a compliment considering that his was a respectable, well-established business. I told him that we would think about it and stay in touch, then we exchanged cards and said goodbye. Our sales for that day exceeded our expectations by far; we covered the entire cost of the stand and earned a slight profit. We were looking forward to our next day.

The second day commenced on Saturday at noon, so Transito and I arrived at ten o'clock in the morning to prepare the stand; Susan and Rosa would arrive closer to the event's starting time, but they would be available to receive messages from us should anything have been left behind. Although business was very brisk at first, things began to slow down between two and two thirty in the afternoon; I started to think that we would be hard pressed to sell at the same level we did the previous night.

Again many of our new friends and acquaintances were coming over to say hello and purchase our products; at around two thirty in the afternoon, Mary Ellen and Jordi dropped by. After about five minutes of small talk, they asked whether they could help us sell; we consented, and for the next three hours I saw them demonstrate incredible salesmanship. As Mary Ellen went behind the counter and put on one of our spare aprons, Jordi worked the crowd like an experienced hand; in a great display of teamwork, he would engage any passersby in discussions about our products while Mary Ellen called more people over to our stand, speaking either English or Spanish depending on the clientele. They were attracting quite a few people to the stand; Susan and I tried to keep pace with the tastings, but very quickly gave up on individual presentation, instead filling plates with six or seven pieces of bread with one type of olive oil each to create a self-serve counter. People took to it immediately, tasting all the oils and ordering bottles of the ones that they liked best. Rosa handled the cash and the bagging, and Transito sat on a wall behind our stand; since he is always security conscious, I am sure he was watching over the money and the inventory.

At about five thirty in the evening, Mary Ellen and Jordi said goodbye. Susan and I were exhausted; although we valiantly tried to stay focused, by six o'clock we needed a break. Taking off our aprons, we asked Rosa and Transito to run the stand while we went for a walk and indulged in the food that was being offered. Not fifteen minutes had passed when we glanced back at the counter and were amazed to see Rosa and Transito attending to at least three couples; when we had left, we had thought we were done for the day, and yet business was speeding up again. Looking around, we observed that even though the crowds had diminished substantially, our counter continued to be as busy as it had been at around two thirty; Susan and I decided to sit on a bench roughly sixty feet away from the stand, where we would have a clear view of what was going on.

What we observed was eye opening: Rosa and Transito had turned into a version of Mary Ellen and Jordi. Transito was talking to the people, Rosa was diligently presenting the tastings and they were both calling people over to the stand; it was an amazing and very pleasing sight. As the pace started quickening, we felt that we needed to give them a hand; after arriving at the stand, I asked Transito why they were so busy. He replied, "When Mary Ellen and Jordi were here, we observed. Now that they're gone, we're doing what they were doing." When we closed the stand by eight o'clock that night, Susan was electrified; upon returning home, she counted the receipts for the day and found that we had done incredibly well.

The next day was crazy, both literally and logistically; it is a Sunday in SMA that happens once each year, called *el Día de los Locos* (the Day of the Crazies). This holiday is sort of like Halloween in that both children and adults dress up in all kinds of costumes and parade through the town for about two hours starting at approximately eleven o'clock in the morning, but they throw candy at onlookers instead of receive it. Because of the parade, we had heavy crowds at our stand from the time we opened at noon until we finished at six o'clock in the evening.

We accomplished quite a bit at this event; it maximized our exposure not only to the public but also to key chefs and restaurants. Everyone was totally surprised to learn that we were making olive oil in SMA; more importantly, they felt proud when they heard it, but not as proud as Rosa and Transito when after a while they began bragging to people that they were the ones who really made the oil. I loved that the staff was taking ownership. Meeting the various chefs was also a very positive experience; many of them became not only friends but also business partners. Our relationship with two in particular, Armando Prats and Leo De La Sierra, grew especially close; we had gotten to know them at our *comidas* when they accompanied our friend Dr. Barrera. During the event, both of them were cooking with our olive oil and telling people about it, so that we felt like contributing members of the SMA community; they also suggested that we participate in an upcoming October event called Five Chefs, so I made a mental note for future reference.

Gil and Rebecca orchestrated more events in June; each time I went to Zandunga, Gil would introduce me to someone who had been robbed by the same two men who had robbed us. I found it interesting that all the victims lived in the countryside and were many miles apart from each other; it seemed to me as if someone other than the robbers was doing the reconnaissance. One victim even told me that the robbers had stolen his iPad and had been dumb enough to take pictures with it; since the iPad had been synced with the victim's computer, the pictures had been transmitted to it.

I was fed up with Mexico; since we had already arranged for a five-day trip to Florida in June, we decided to extend it to six weeks and get away from it all. I was confused and conflicted: I loved our property in Mexico substantially more than I had twelve months earlier and passionately adored our new occupation, which had been the best I had ever had, but I also hated Mexico more than I ever thought I would!

Gil was closing Zandunga for six weeks; he wanted to replace the shade cloth with a sheet-metal roof. We sent our staff there to work with Gil, and he paid for the materials; sure enough, during the six weeks we were away Transito and his son brought all the necessary equipment, and together with Gil's crew they saw the project to its conclusion. Even though they were there for most of the time, everything that we expected to be done at our farm and house was also carried out with no complaints.

After saying our goodbyes to Transito and his family, we departed for Florida on June 24. We flew to Orlando, rented a car and drove to the home of Susan's sister in Matlacha as our initial stop on a six-week tour that would span the eastern coast of the US.

The trip had originally been planned by my son-in-law Vinny, who had decided to give my daughter Jana a surprise fortieth birthday party that would be celebrated in the Florida Keys, starting with a special surprise greeting at Alabama Jack's, a well-known biker hangout, just before entering Key Largo. Although my daughter's birthday is in March, Vinny had really wanted to keep her totally in the dark by having the party in June.

We, along with my daughter Lara, my son-in-law Camilo and many of their friends, came to Alabama Jack's at the appointed time, and when Jana and Vinny entered, we all yelled "Surprise!" Poor Jana nearly collapsed! And thus began four festive days of celebration; seeing my daughters go biking together was an incredibly satisfying experience. The party was a lot of fun and too short; it will always be remembered. While we were celebrating Jana's birthday, we stayed at a wonderful seaside motel near Marathon Key, fifty-three miles from Key West; Susan and I would have our morning coffee as we sat by the water's edge and just stared out at the ocean. These four days were exactly what we needed; we relaxed, did not think much about anything and simply enjoyed our family and their friends.

As we headed north from the Keys, we saw a sign for an olive-oil shop but were going too fast to stop and check it out; at the spur of the moment, we made a U-turn and visited the shop. Susan and I smiled as we took in the atmosphere, products and look of the place, focusing on every detail and dreaming of having a lifestyle like this. Instinctively, we knew we were inside a shop affiliated with Veronica Foods, the same outfit that supplied the store in SMA; when we inspected the front and back of one of the bottles, our hunch was confirmed. This shop's product offerings were much more extensive than our competitor's at home; we bought some oil there and continued to Matlacha, arriving on June 30.

It is amazing how a very small thing can have a major impact on one's life; that quick U-turn changed our demeanor and the purpose of our trip. We decided to conduct a mission to find out everything we possibly could about olive oil as we drove up the East Coast to New York.

What a month! I started it feeling completely empty and ended it full of hope and optimism.

Our East Coast Olive Oil Odyssey: July 2015

Matlacha is part of the Fort Meyers–Cape Coral greater metropolitan area; located on a small island, this community has a population of about one thousand people. Susan and I have had an incredible number of great experiences; one of our best was living in a waterfront house in New Jersey, where we had our own dock and boat behind the house. We loved being on the water, and Susan's sister Ruth and her brother-in-law Dennis's house is right on the water.

For that reason, heading to Matlacha was magical to us. After arriving at the house, I immediately began to look for olive-oil stores near us; I located one not far away, and Susan and I drove to it. Walking into the shop, we found ourselves inside another independently owned store supplied by Veronica Foods; as we were purchasing more olive oil, I was thinking that Veronica Foods was spreading like wildfire throughout the country.

When we returned to the house, I decided to see whether the two stores where we had stopped had websites; sure enough, they had websites with the same look and feel, as if they had been built using a template. Through my research, I became very familiar with the types of outfits affiliated with Veronica Foods. Not that I had anything against these stores—on the contrary, I thought they created a wonderful shopping environment—but I wanted to expand our knowledge and experience base, and so we determined that we did not need to visit any more shops associated with this supplier. We surfed the Internet for other places we could find on our trip that was related to olive oil.

Because of our plant and tree nursery experience, we were surprised to find that olives were being grown in Florida; we called an outfit located in mid-northern Florida and made an appointment to visit on July 3. Unfortunately, we missed our appointment because we had grossly underestimated how long it would take us to get there; however, we did see some trees being replanted and a building being constructed that would house an oil press. We were shown only a small section of the grove, but it was sufficient for us to determine that the trees were flourishing. Moreover, we learned that land in northern Florida was much cheaper than in SMA. The trip lasted an entire day, but we managed to arrive back at the house in time to enjoy cocktails with the family at sunset.

The rest of our stay in Matlacha was spent relaxing, enjoying our time with the family and quietly celebrating the passage of the first year of our business plan, as well as Susan's birthday on July 7. I continued surfing the Internet and plotting what we had dubbed our East Coast Olive Oil Odyssey. Our next scheduled stop was Marietta, Georgia, to visit Lara and her family; I found two olive-oil producers in Georgia, and one of them was close to the route we would follow to Lara's house. We made a reservation at a hotel in Valdosta, Georgia, as well as an appointment to tour the producer's facilities.

We departed from Matlacha early on the morning of July 8, and by three o'clock in the afternoon we had arrived at our hotel in Valdosta. I was looking forward to this stopover, since it was my first visit to a truly commercial operation for the production of olive oil.

We met our guide at a local art shop and proceeded to the field and processing plant about a thirty-minute drive away from the town. The people who had started the olive-growing and -processing business were well-established professional farmers; they had set aside about one hundred acres for the cultivation of olives. Their project was under five years old.

When we arrived, I was surprised by how tall the trees were growing; after two years, the trees were nearly six feet high, and by four years their height had reached almost ten feet as they approached full production capacity. They were mostly of the "Arbequina" variety; clearly, these people had finished experimenting and were focused on expanding rapidly.

The olives were mechanically harvested, collecting immediately into a container pulled by a tractor; as one container filled, another took its place. Each full container was then towed to the processing plant and dumped into a vat that machine washes the olives to begin the oil-making process.

Their mill had a very modern centrifuge press by Alfa Laval, one of the top global mill manufacturers. Untouched by human hands, the olives entered one end of the machine and came out the other end as oil; the wasted pulp and crushed stones were diverted to a side container. Obviously, we could only imagine the process, since harvest would not be beginning until late October.

The tour guide had briefly mentioned a Swedish retiree who was the first to experiment with cultivating and processing olives mechanically; he lived just outside Tallahassee, Florida. When I also heard that he was selling his small farm with established olive trees, as soon as I had returned to the hotel I frantically searched until I found not only press coverage about the gentleman but also the sale listing for the house. However, Susan was not interested at all in the property, refusing even to go look at it; she had fervently hated living in Florida. Keeping all options open, I also researched real estate values in southern Georgia.

We departed from Valdosta early on July 9, following our well-established routine; during a typical road trip, we either had a light breakfast at the hotel if available or went to the first McDonald's we saw and got coffee and an Egg McMuffin for each of us, seldom stopping for lunch. When we arrived in Marietta, a suburb of Atlanta, at around four o'clock in the afternoon, my grandchildren Addy and Sebastian were home from school. This was unusual because Lara had a full schedule of activities for them ranging from ice-skating lessons for Addy to the YMCA for Sebastian. Our evening was spent catching up and playing with the kids.

We got up on Friday morning fully recharged and ready to handle some personal business at the local office of the Social Security Administration. Afterward, we all went to the local Whole Foods Market; Susan looked for meats to grill, I checked out the olive oils and we treated the kids and ourselves to gelato. The next six days were full of flying a new remote-control plane at the local schoolyard, basketball at the YMCA, Ping-Pong and trips to Whole Foods for gelato; during the evenings, the whole family watched "I Love Lucy" shows.

We managed to fit a couple of olive-oil side trips into our schedule as well. In Atlanta, we visited a wonderful olive-oil shop that was different from the others we had seen in that it did not look like a franchise. At a Saturday market in Marietta, we purchased some olive oil supposedly from Uruguay, but we found that it did not taste very good.

Our stay in Marietta ended too quickly, but we knew that we would stop by again on the way to Orlando for our return flight to Mexico. Next we headed for Washington, DC, to see Minerva; this visit was typically for one night. We arrived in time to treat her to dinner at a restaurant located in one of the huge malls in

Tysons Corner, Virginia. As we were going up an escalator, we noticed a very large olive-oil display with many fustis; even from a distance we could tell that Veronica Foods had supplied it. Not wanting to disrupt our time with my sister, we proceeded to the restaurant; however, there was a wait time of about thirty minutes, so Susan took the opportunity to get a closer look at the oil shop. She came back in fifteen minutes and reported that while the store was closed, she had confirmed that it was a Veronica Foods affiliate.

We departed on the next day for our five-hour road trip to New York City. Staying at Grace's was a lot of fun, with great food and discussions. However, we also had the worst night's sleep possible; the bed was extremely uncomfortable and the street noise in New York was louder than what we had experienced in any other city in the world. Nevertheless, we endured the torment, and yes, we found one olive-oil store with two different locations; we liked the store and got several good ideas for our business. When we went to Fairway Market near Grace's apartment, I was surprised to see various kinds of cured olives being offered and sold directly from *cubetas*. On Saturday, we drove to Jana's house, and after visiting a local farm market we had a cookout in the backyard.

We started our reverse trek on July 26, then spent two days in Marietta. Realizing that we could not fit all our purchases into our bags, we bought two large bags to pack what we would be taking with us; even with the additional bags, we had to leave behind a bag full of clothes, which we would pick up during our next trip. Our last stop was in Orlando, where we visited our niece and her family.

We returned to our home late in the afternoon on July 30; we were greeted not only by our dogs but also by a flyover of the International Space Station, which was a wonderful sight. Watching the full moon rise on the eastern horizon made our arrival at Luna Serena very special as well.

Although I was still unhappy living in Mexico, I truly wanted to give it a fair shot; I had realized that for the last forty-five years, I had been on a plane at least every eight weeks, and I was tired, turning seventy years old and ready to settle down. However, I also knew that as long as I kept going back every eight weeks, I would be reluctant to cut free from the US and fully commit to Mexico; I would always be yearning to return. As I had come to this conclusion, I had made a promise to myself that I would never leave Mexico for at least twelve months and preferably eighteen months. I confided all this to Susan.

I had realized as well that the emotional scars from the robbery would stay with me no matter where I lived; yes, I had to become more vigilant, but I also needed to keep my life moving forward.

Turning Seventy: August 2015

Our first event at Zandunga after returning from our trip was on August 2. The work done by Transito and Gil's crew was outstanding: the area previously covered by shade cloth now had a full metal roof with plastic laminas strategically placed to create natural lighting; it easily added another one thousand five hundred square feet of space. Gil's crew had also made tables and benches from pallets, which gave the space a nice funky look. Additionally, the taco and quesadilla stations were moved to the rear of the new area, right next to our counter, so that everyone getting something to eat had to pass by us; the impact on our sales was immediate.

Our stand near town was generating a small profit, which was much more than we ever expected. Susan began making sure the stand was adequately stocked.

"Manzanilla" is the olive we grow and process that is harvested earliest; beginning in mid-August, some of these olives are picked green, while others are left on the tree to ripen. Over a period of approximately eight weeks, the olives are picked at various stages of ripeness, primarily for use as a table olive.

However, in 2014 we had produced oil from this olive as a way to fine-tune our equipment; at the time, we had concluded that it was not economical. Afterward, a visiting friend knowledgeable about olive oil had tasted it and loved its unique piquant taste; when he had inquired about the retail price of the oil, I had told him that I would not be making the oil for sale because it would have to sold at a very high price in order to make a profit, and the market would not bear it. Pressing further, he had stated that he would pay three hundred dollars for a bottle of the oil, adding that the price would be a better value than the approximately one hundred dollars commonly paid for a bottle of very good wine at a restaurant. "After all," he had reasoned, "the oil would last much longer."

Therefore, on August 10 we began our curing and pressing season. Starting with three hundred kilograms of green "Manzanilla," we brine cured half for a green table olive and pressed the remainder for oil. We obtained eight liters of the oil, and it tasted excellent; I had it bottled immediately and kept in a cabinet.

A significant event in August was the vendimia at a new venue, Vinedos San Miguel; it was the first event held there and attended by more than one thousand people. We were excited to be part of the affair. As it turned out, the labor, as well as the personal time and effort, that we expended did not make this an immediately profitable venture, but as with all our events the benefits came much later; the key thing we learned was that was we needed to be more discriminating about the types events we selected. The main focus of the vendimia was wine, food, dancing and fun; our sales approach, on the other hand, emphasized presentation and education about olive oil, which apparently required more time than the vendimia attendees were willing to grant.

Turning seventy years old was not a big affair to me; I was too busy to even reflect on it. Susan knew that I did not like to have birthday parties, so she did not plan one; I must say, though, that it was a lot of fun to receive a surprise birthday cake, which was shared by nearly one hundred people at a Sunday event in Zandunga.

We had projected a heavier olive-processing period than we had had in 2014, so we built two additional presses for a total of six. By the end of August, the oil olives had started trickling in and we had begun pressing and storing them; our goal was to make one thousand liters of olive oil by the end of the 2015 season.

Should our anticipated sales for 2015 be achieved, we would be selling two hundred liters of the current production, and so we estimated that we would eventually require storage capacity for eight hundred liters; to accomplish this, we would have to double our current storage capacity. I spent quite a bit of time forecasting things like that, projecting supply needs and calculating yields, all of which were becoming more complex since our product line had been expanded to vinegars and jellies.

Susan was busy keeping the office supplied with the proper label paper and ensuring that we had a sufficient number of printed labels; in the process, we destroyed two printers. Finding enough of the appropriate ink cartridges also became problematic, due to their scarcity in SMA.

The amount of work for the staff also dramatically increased; fortunately, our staff did a fantastic job orchestrating everything. As shown by the following list of their duties, this was no easy task:

Feeding dogs
Cleaning the house every day (sweeping, mopping, windows)
Processing new olives
Bottling and labeling olive oil for sale
Preparing herb olives, packaging and labeling
Preparing vinegar-brine olives, packaging and labeling
Picking fruit from trees
Making cider
Starting new vinegar
Measuring vinegar acidity
Pasteurizing vinegars
Bottling and labeling vinegars
Cleaning sheep pens and horse stalls daily
Feeding sheep, horses and chickens
Taking horses and sheep to and from pasture
Periodically fertilizing trees
Watering trees
Vehicle maintenance as needed
Harvesting vegetables

Making jellies
Keeping town store supplied
Preparing products for sale at Zandunga
Manning Zandunga stand

This list does not include everything, but it illustrates the level of activity in our growing business.

Hot-air Balloons and Organic Farming: September 2015

As all this activity was taking place from day to day and from month to month, we still had to cope with the unexpected.

During seasons of heavy tourism, a fleet of six or seven hot-air balloons visits SMA. It is not unusual to see the balloons rising from the valley below our mountain; I believe the balloons start on the other side of town and gently float over the picturesque town of SMA. Normally, they begin their ascent minutes before the expected sunrise time, so that the passengers get a wonderful view of the dawn as well as of SMA. As the balloons drift over the town, they also pass by our area. Having ascended nearly seven thousand five hundred feet, the balloons are only a few hundred feet above us; sometimes, we can even make out the faces of the passengers. Our dogs' keen sense of hearing alerts them when a balloon is going airborne in the valley; they incessantly run around the property and bark at this unexpected alien form.

On one early September morning, our dogs were barking more loudly than usual; when I went out the back door, I discovered that a hot-air balloon was hovering less than twenty feet over our grove. The pilot of the balloon was frantically yelling something at me; I assumed he was saying that he wanted to land on our estate, so I shouted back that he should touch down on our neighbor's property and frenziedly pointed in that direction. I was concerned that should he alight here, our dogs would attack as a pack; the pilot must have gotten my message, since the balloon started very slowly inching upward and heading away from our land. Calming down, I reached for the camera on my phone and was able to take some pretty fantastic pictures.

As stated earlier, we had become one of the founding members of the Guanajuato Olive Growers Association. Over a year had passed before we started having regular meetings and setting the agenda, but our small group was keen on planting more trees. A consultant was hired to work with members of the association, providing advice on the cultivation of the olive trees; the first time he came to us, he was extremely kind not to belittle our four hundred ugly eight-year-old trees. On subsequent visits, however, he was less gracious, suggesting that we take them out; I refused to do so. We were already on a program of planting additional trees; within the next twelve months, we would have nearly one thousand two hundred trees planted. I was thinking many steps ahead of the other members of the association; their main focus was growing trees, whereas our objective was to create a tourism destination, which would require us to attend to all our products and build our brand, not just develop our olive grove.

Our sales at Zandunga jumped again. Apparently, while we were away Rebecca had asked Transito to bring her some of our organic eggs, which were gaining a reputation as the best eggs in SMA; Rebecca had then told Transito that he could sell the eggs if he wished, and it was not long before the egg business took off. The eggs in town cost five pesos, or about thirty cents each; Transito charged only three pesos, and they sold like hot cakes. I supported the pricing strategy because we wanted people to eventually visit our farm to see our chickens and buy our eggs along with all our other products; my estimate was that at worst we would break even and still enjoy the most delicious eggs we ever tasted.

It is common knowledge that planting vegetables and trees is not just about putting seeds or seedlings in the ground; they have to be nurtured by feeding and watering them at the appropriate times and with the right substances. To that end, we developed our own organic fertilizer from the manure of the horses, sheep and chickens. Obviously, this was not something that I had learned during my forty-five years on Madison Avenue; however, over the years of owning our farm in Mexico we had acquired a fairly extensive library of books about animal husbandry.

The manure was collected daily and taken to a far corner of the property, where it was left to dry. Over quite a long period of time, we had accumulated a very good working pile of dry manure that had been consistently utilized to fertilize our trees, vegetables and flowers after sifting it through screen mesh in order to create a finer material. While this method had sufficed for many years, we needed to find a way to supplement the feeding process. In addition, the use of pesticides and herbicides was not allowed on our property, which obviously resulted in lower fruit and vegetable yields; producing on a commercial level would require more efficiency in this regard.

Therefore, we hired a consultant to provide us with advice on the organic management of our place. Our consultant conducted soil and leaf analyses of our various trees, and within two weeks after his first visit we had a range of organic products that would serve as fertilizers, herbicides and pesticides. Transito and I received the appropriate training on how to apply these products, even though any errors in application would not result in damage to crops, animals or people. Our extensive system of drip irrigation, supported by three water tanks that each held ten thousand liters, aided in the distribution of liquid organic fertilizer to supplement our usual solid fertilizer.

As the olive harvest intensified, so did our processing; our olive suppliers were having a bumper crop. We noticed that some of the olives appeared to be of different varieties; although we easily identified the "Manzanilla" and "Arbequina" olives, we were receiving other olives that were unlabeled but clearly distinguishable by size and color. When we kept the varieties separate to find out what the resulting oils would taste like, we were surprised to discover that they had distinctive hues and flavors; we then stored and labeled each of these oils with a description of the olive as well as the date when it was pressed.

September would prove to be a month of incredibly heavy olive production. Our increased processing capacity, as well as the experience we had gained, allowed us to process at least three thousand kilograms of olives and to press over six hundred liters of olive oil, which was fifty percent more than we had made during our entire first season in 2014.

I suspected the weak link in our process was the industrial meat grinder that crushed the olives; by midmonth it was no longer operating, so we took it apart and found that one of the worm gears had been stripped as a result of the heavy use. Fortunately, I was able to contact the distributor in Mexico; within two days, we received two replacement parts, one for immediate installation and the other as a spare.

Realizing that we could not be without a means to grind olives, we started searching for an alternative method; the industrial meat grinder was very effective, but we did not want to spend one thousand dollars for a spare. Our solution was uniquely Mexican; for less than three hundred dollars, we were able to obtain a brand-new grinder normally used to make corn flour for tortillas. The grinder's working parts, other than an electric motor, were a set of grinding stones that did a wonderful job of crushing the olives; though it was not perfect, it served as a backup grinder in the event that our main one became inoperative.

A Big Event: October 2015

We were close to achieving our goal of producing one thousand liters of olive oil; at this point, we needed to find a stronger sales outlet than Zandunga or our small olive-oil stand near town, which was supporting a miniscule number of sales.

At the beginning of the month, Susan and I sat down to evaluate our current situation, focusing on our strengths and weaknesses. Although our products were very good, our packaging gave the impression that we were amateurs; we still had not found a suitable dark-colored bottle, and our labels did not evoke a high-quality image. Selling our increased supply of olive oils would require a professional appearance for our products, but our business looked more like a mom-and-pop operation.

We also believed that many of our day-to-day issues should be handled by someone familiar with how businesses operate within Mexico, since we were having difficulty finding the most basic business supplies. Our immediate world was limited to SMA, and we did not really know much about obtaining business support within its confines; at times, I even struggled with the language. Moreover, we did not understand how to navigate in the nearby cities of Querétaro and Celaya. For all these reasons, Susan and I instinctively realized that we needed office staff; our experience in managing large advertising teams had taught us that in order to think beyond the mundane and focus on growing our little operation, we must delegate some of our tasks to an employee who can do them better than we can. The ideal solution, we concluded, was to hire a young Mexican university graduate to help us who speaks both English and Spanish.

Earlier that year, we had given Dr. Barrera a surprise birthday party, and his three daughters had been present for the occasion; one of them, Marisol, was a budding young photographer living and working in Mexico City. We had asked Marisol whether she would be interested in doing some photo shoots for us, since we suspected that sometime in the future we would need professionally rendered pictures of our products. When Marisol came to visit with us, she was expecting a discussion about this assignment.

The more we spoke with Marisol, the more Susan and I believed that she might be able to help us. When Marisol told us that she was primarily engaged in photography during weekends and was actively seeking employment from Monday to Friday, Susan and I offered her a job on the spot. Recognizing that she had to be based in Mexico, we hoped that she would spend one or two weeks per month with us in SMA and the rest of the time working remotely from Mexico City; she accepted the position, starting immediately.

Her first assignment was to go with us to a venue outside SMA, where a press conference was being held for an upcoming event called Five Chefs. During the previous month, we had contracted to have a stand at the event, which was projected to have approximately seven hundred people in attendance; Our cost for the stand was rather steep at ten thousand pesos for the stand; we had paid the rather steep price of ten thousand pesos for the space in order to become an official sponsor. There was considerable press coverage prior to the event, and we were included.

The event featured five SMA chefs, five national chefs and five international chefs, who were grouped into five teams preparing food for five distinct culinary areas of Mexico. Located about a fifteen-minute drive away from the town of SMA, the venue was spectacular. Our position within the event was excellent; not only did we get pre-event press coverage, but we also provided the olive oil that all the chefs cooked with.

The stands, made from wooden pallets and arranged to resemble a series of small village shops, were located on the perimeter of a very large hall. In the center of the area were seventy tables seating ten people each. At one end of the hall was a huge stage lined with shops on both sides, and at the other was a set of stairs leading to the terrace where the band played; a water fountain cascaded from the terrace down to the main floor. Clearly, this event was going to be a show that would attract people from neighboring states as well as Mexico City.

The promoters of the show had grown up in an olive-growing region of Mexico; they hinted that they had consumed a lot of olive oil during their early childhood. Upon tasting our oil, they became nostalgic; we instantly won them over. They started bringing many people to our stand, including local and state officials; we made many acquaintances who would prove to be influential in the development of our business during months to come.

Our sales during the event did not recoup the cost of the stand. In retrospect, however, the event impacted our business and our lives in many different positive ways; the return on our original investment of ten thousand pesos has been tremendous.

Marisol had a wedding photo shoot scheduled during the weekend of our event, so she could not attend. During the week after the event, she began urging Susan and me to join social media; Susan and I had resisted getting involved in any type of social media, but Marisol convinced us that we needed to do so in order to improve our sales and our image. By the end of the week, we each had Facebook pages; little did any of us realize how something that seemed so inconsequential at the time would impact our lives in a major positive way.

Marisol was given some key tasks to help us achieve our objectives, and she put her heart into them; over the following week, she listed our cottage on Airbnb and began to assist us in finding appropriate bottles and making our labels more professional.

Looking for ways to expand our business base, we hoped to be able to sell online; our first step in this direction was identifying the most economical way to ship our products to other parts of Mexico. With Marisol's help, we shipped two bottles of our oil to her through a popular express-delivery system in Mexico; she received the bottles, but we were dismayed to find out that the cheapest shipping cost was over eighty percent of the retail price for the products shipped. Our search for a more inexpensive method has proved futile.

At the end of the month, we received the oil-testing equipment we had ordered two months earlier; we wanted to verify that our olive oil qualified as extra-virgin. Oil with this classification must not exceed an acidity level of four-fifths of a percent, and our oil had half a percent; happy to have confirmed our expectation, we concluded that my reading was paying off, as this level of acidity is achieved with proper processing and handling.

Monarch Butterflies: November 2015

On Sunday, November 1, the event at Zandunga was totally sold out. At this point, Transito and Rosa were able to run the counter on their own; Transito's egg business continued to augment our sales. Susan and I decided to take the afternoon off, go dancing and enjoy a couple glasses of tequila.

As the event neared its end, people began to exchange parting words. Susan, seeing some dear friends leaving, decided to go over and bid them farewell. At the time, we were sitting on a wall at least five feet high by a terrace with a table in front of us; I rose to let her walk around the table and proceed down the terrace to where our friends were standing. In a split second, Susan swung her feet over the other side of the wall and prepared to jump down; I warned, "You should not be doing that," to which she replied, "I can handle it." Then she leaped and hit the ground hard, breaking her fall with her left hand, but she got up, brushed herself off and approached our friends to say goodbye. As she came back to where I was waiting, I noticed that she was discreetly holding her wrist; when I asked her how her wrist felt, she replied, "It hurts." We finished the day and returned home.

On the next day, Susan was in much greater pain. I took her to the doctor, and x-rays confirmed that she had broken her wrist. Surgery was scheduled for the following day.

Susan is incredibly healthy; she seldom needs to go see a doctor. In fact, prior to this incident she had not had a medical appointment for at least four years, which is a good thing because Susan is panic stricken if anybody approaches her with a needle; she is totally incapable of accepting any type of injection.

At a meeting with the surgeon on the day before the operation, the procedure had been explained to her. After arriving at the hospital early in the morning for the procedure, Susan was told something different than before. Unbeknownst to the doctor, Susan had meticulously prepared to accept what was going to happen, spending the entire night playing out the procedure in her mind over and over again. When informed of the altered procedure, she totally freaked out and fled from the hospital, cursing and yelling in a manner I had never before seen her do; she is normally a very calm, reserved person. Dr. Barrera quickly followed, trying to convince her that it was a minor, inconsequential change made by the surgeon, but Susan would have none of it and said that she refused to undergo the surgery.

In the end, she finally agreed to the procedure only if she was given laughing gas for the anesthesia, as it did not involve a needle. Apparently, she was not an easy person to handle on the operating table; while she was recuperating, Dr. Barrera came over to me and said, "She is a witch."

Finally, I was allowed to see her in the recuperation room. Susan was lying on a gurney, covered by a blanket; underneath, she was wearing jeans, sneakers and a tank top. She had an IV in her right arm and was sporting a solid cast from her wrist almost to her shoulder. Not yet fully awake, she groggily looked at her cast, then said, "What is this? I want it off. I want out of here" and sat up angrily. Luckily, an astute attendant quickly removed the IV; otherwise, Susan would have ripped it all off. As she ran out of the hospital and to our car, I grabbed her shirt and told the doctor that I needed to get her home and calm her down; I would be back to sign any remaining paperwork and to pay for her visit.

I drove Susan home and put her in bed, where she slept for the remainder of the day. It took a few days to calm her down because she was still in pain, but fortunately Luna Serena is an incredibly tranquil place to recuperate; life quickly returned to normalcy.

Finca Luna Serena is located at an altitude of six thousand eight hundred twenty-four feet above sea level (though I like to round it to seven thousand feet), and it is not the highest point in our area; the mountains less than four miles south of us have elevations of more than nine thousand feet, and the mountains to our north are a few hundred feet higher than our place. There are no taller mountains east of us, and to the west our mountain sharply declines, giving us an unobstructed view of the valley below; to say that most of our sunsets and sunrises are spectacular would be an understatement. Less than half a mile from us is El Charco, a natural sanctuary with botanical gardens. Migrating birds often make stopovers on our property and fill our farm with their wonderful music.

Susan can confirm that I tend to walk past many things without perceiving them; because I am usually deep in thought, at times I seem angry or absentminded and even forget to greet people. On November 5, I sat down in my office, then noticed that I had left my filled coffee mug at the main house, so I went back to get it. As I passed the hedges and entered the front courtyard, I sensed that I had missed something, but I had no idea what; I turned around and stopped in an area thirty feet away. At first glance, I saw nothing out of the ordinary, but when I looked more closely at the weeping pepper tree to my right, I observed that its leaves appeared to be shimmering; I very quickly realized that they were not leaves but thousands of MONARCH BUTTERFLIES!

My first instinct was to yell for Susan, but I was afraid that it would scare them. Although I wanted to run over to her, I was concerned that it might startle them, so I softly walked to the house and got Susan to come quietly, leaving the dogs behind. The monarchs covered most of our trees; some of them folded their wings, others kept them open and several were flying away. Not long prior to this incident, I had read about their migration to various sites in the states of Mexico and Michoacán. Obviously, they were resting overnight at

Finca Luna Serena! Their favorite tree is eucalyptus, of which we have many different varieties. I took out my iPhone and started filming and taking pictures. By nine thirty that morning, all the butterflies were gone.

I read more about their migration and was pretty giddy all day. At around six o'clock that evening, monarch butterflies started arriving and alighting on our trees; I took more pictures. On the next morning, I sat and watched them wake, open their wings, warm up and fly away. This went on for a total of six days; I posted the pictures on Facebook, sent them to friends and hoped that the monarchs would be back again the following year.

The olive harvest ended in November. Most people believe that there are two types of olives, one green and the other black; in reality, there is only one type of olive, and the difference between green and black ones is simply how ripe they are—as olives ripen, their color gradually changes from green to black. Almost all the olives harvested in November were black. Susan decided to try curing approximately one hundred kilograms of ripe olives in sea salt; the olives were layered with salt in a container, and the process was complete after about five weeks. We then washed the olives and sun dried them for five days; half were packed in vacuum bags and half in olive oil. At the time, I did not think there would be much demand for this product, but it would turn out to be one of our most popular differentiated products!

Living at a working farm has many ups and downs. There are moments of ecstasy, such as the birth of a lamb, chicks hatching and even the appearance of natural phenomena like the monarch butterflies' stopovers; however, there are also some very sad occasions, and to me one of the worst is when an animal is injured or dies. On November 16, Versario, our full-bred dorper ram, passed away from bloat, which is a condition in the digestive system caused by excessive generation of stomach gases that the animal is unable to expel; it can be deadly if it is not detected early or treated correctly. Even though our vet quickly came to our aid, we could not save the ram's life.

Versario had grown to be a champion ram; he weighed nearly three hundred pounds and had sired many lambs. However, to put it kindly, he was a really ornery son of a bitch; he loved to gore people, and he could inflict some serious damage due to his size. Fortunately, I was the only one who actually experienced this behavior; after my first incident, people were forewarned. On one particular day quite a few months prior to his death, he had attacked me from the side and given me a limp for over a month; nevertheless, I loved the guy, and his passing devastated me.

Fortunately, when we had acquired Vieja, a full-bred Katahdin sheep, she had been pregnant with and subsequently given birth to a full-bred Katahdin ram, which we had called Horny because he constantly wanted to mount any ewes that were around. We had kept him separate from Versario because they would start butting heads on sight. Horny had grown as big as Versario, but had a much kinder, gentler disposition; he became our new stud. When we lost several more sheep during the month of November, we surmised that there was a problem with their feed.

Susan was scheduled to leave for New York to spend Thanksgiving with Grace. One week prior to her departure, one of our chef acquaintances suggested that we consider getting a permanent stand in a new market being erected inside a building at a prime location in town. We went to visit it and spoke with the landlord; having fallen in love with the idea and the location, we wanted to move quickly.

Our search for accountants and lawyers had finally paid off, and we had not had to look far; Dr. Barrera had been keeping an eye out for promising leads and recommended a highly qualified group. A week earlier, we had signed on with a senior partner who would be handling our taxes and legal affairs; we sent him the lease documents for the new stand and signed the lease after his quick review, then paid the funds required to finalize the contract. We were truly excited, as we thought this was the answer to our prayers for a high-volume sales center.

Prior to her departure, Susan insisted that her cast be taken off even though she was supposed to wear it for several more weeks; though the doctors refused to do it themselves, they did allow a capable assistant to do as

Susan wished. Susan had purchased a more comfortable one called an air cast; upon removal of the permanent cast, she put on the air cast and walked out of the hospital. A few days later, she was headed for New York.

While she was away, I did a lot of planning and reading; I was continuing to educate myself about all the products that we were making. In one book, I came across a section about a producer in Spain whose olive oil was being sold for ten times more than that of his competitors because his method produced superior oil; I researched this method and concluded that the oil we had been collecting prior to pressing was very similar. We had managed to obtain nearly twenty liters of oil this way during the 2015 harvest season, then bottled the oil, labeling it as "Reserva de la Familia"; it was intended for either our own use or gifts to friends. I sent a note to Susan in New York, asking her to pick up and bring to Mexico the oil that the book mentions.

My Thanksgiving was a very quiet affair. Susan was in New York, and it is a regular workday to for our Mexican staff; nevertheless, I asked María to butcher one of our tom turkeys in keeping with the tradition. We put the turkey in brine overnight, and María cooked it the next day; it turned out delicious.

Broken Promise: December 2015

When Susan arrived from her trip to New York, I was having a meeting with two chefs at our home. Susan had brought the special olive oil with her from two producers; I went into the kitchen and asked Susan to help me conduct a blind taste test of these two oils and the oil that we had made. We had the chefs taste the trio and choose the one that they thought was best, and we were extremely pleased when they both selected our oil. After they left, the oil was rebottled into our custom-made talavera bottles and sealed; we planned to sell this oil at double the price of regular oil.

Susan had finally found a label printer for us in town. Our logo was changed to a full moon with an olive tree in its center on a black background. At last, our labels looked professional; the front panel contained our logo, the product description, our name and our address, and the nutrition information was on the rear panel. We no longer had to use our homemade labels.

For the last three weeks, we had been busy building our inventory for the opening of the new market where our store would be located, which was scheduled to take place during the week before Christmas. When Susan and I paid a visit to the locale, we came to the conclusion that it would be a miracle if it opened before the middle of January; however, we remained hopeful that there might be a trick up someone's sleeve that would have it ready in time for the holidays.

At midmonth, we got a call from the landlord requesting a meeting; I told Susan that whatever it was, I did not think it was going to be good. Sure enough, at the meeting we were informed that the landlord had encountered a problem with honoring his commitment to us; a contract had previously been signed with one of the other tenants, and the landlord inadvertently had not read its attachment that included a list of products to be exclusively sold by the tenant. The landlord apologetically explained that he could not proceed with our contract.

Containing my anger, I told the landlord that I knew I was within my rights; we could take him to court and cause a lot of trouble for him. I then added that we were not that kind of people; while we were upset, we would rather that he just return the funds.

The landlord felt terrible and apologized profusely. As a last resort, he offered a solution, asking whether I would be interested in selling our olive oil in a jewelry store; there was a very special place that he could show us right away. After walking several blocks with him, we saw a space located deep inside a unique jewelry store made to look like a mine; Susan and I immediately did not like the space, as it had no exposure to external traffic. I told the landlord we would think about it, then we shook hands and left. Susan and I were truly disappointed.

A week later, we were hosting a party at our house with the Barrera family, as well as many of their friends and ours, in honor of our friendship with the Barreras. The chef friends had met with me at our house to plan the menu for the event before they had participated in our taste test. We would be having nearly one hundred guests, and the chefs would be cooking our lamb and turkey for the main course.

As the event was beginning, I was called to our gate to receive some visitors unrelated to the party; they had called a few minutes earlier, inquiring whether they could drop by. It was the landlord from the market and the owner of the jewelry store we had visited, whom I had not met earlier. I spent about half an hour with them and gave them a tasting of our olive oil; impressed, the jewelry storeowner asked that we seriously consider selling our oil in his store, to which I replied that we would think about it and get back to him after the holidays.

Returning to the party, I welcomed all the guests and made a nice speech about the friendship between the Barreras and us. It was a very special and festive occasion.

Our Airbnb listing paid off; we booked the cottage for four days starting on New Year's Eve, our first rental in over five years. We were very pleased that we had commenced another phase of our business plan.

Much had happened in the last twelve months; here are highlights of some of the key events in a whirlwind year:

- We finished 2015 with approximately one thousand liters of olive oil and at least four hundred kilograms of cured olives.
- Our inventory of vinegars, jellies and apple cider was substantial.
- Our farm store did not become the tourism destination we had planned, but we felt confident that it would by 2018.
- We started renting our cottage.
- Gil's place in the countryside became an entertainment venue every Sunday, and we established our business there.
- We were invited to participate in major food events in SMA and had a strong client base for our olive oil.
- Transito sold our eggs at Gil's venue, and many customers said they were the best eggs they ever tasted.
- We went on a road trip during which we flew to Orlando and visited our family along the East Coast.
- We opened a stand to sell our olive oil at a local market; it was run by one of Transito's daughters six days per week.
- We hired accountants and lawyers to attend to the legalities related to our commercial activities.
- Our staff grew from three full-time employees to six full-time and two part-time employees.

- We were selling high-quality sheep that people used for breeding; they did not generate much money, but they paid for their feed. Sheep manure is considered one of the best organic fertilizers; one could say we also started a fertilizer factory.
- We had two additional consultants:
  - One for advising on and supplying organic fertilizer (liquid), organic herbicides and organic pesticides
  - One for providing advice on managing our olive grove
- We were developing a super-intensive olive grove and planted over one thousand trees on our property.
- We harvested nearly four hundred pounds of garlic.
- We were up to seven presses for making the olive oil.

While many positive things happened, we were depressed. We would have very little entertainment during this holiday season; Susan and I were invited to many homes, but we made lame excuses to avoid being around other people. The robbery, the death of our ram Versario, the lease for a store falling through and the stress most of all had taken a lot out of us. My chest pains from costochondritis were relentless, and Susan had a broken wrist on the mend. We did not even bother to see the year through—no Times Square Ball Drop, and no picture slideshow. In my view, everything sucked, and I wanted out of Mexico on New Year's Eve of 2015. Susan sensed my tension and began emotionally withdrawing.

I truly felt that I would not make it through another year; no amount of accomplishment could help me out of the slump.

A Store in SMA: January 2016

On January 1, we woke up with all the hope that a New Year can offer. The staff had the day off. We showered and made our coffee.

While Susan fed the dogs, I stared out the window at the likeness of Christ on our palm tree, which had kept me calm and focused for nine months, and said a few silent prayers as usual. My Christ made me feel better; I believed that my mother and father had sent him as a sign that they were looking after me. As my mood became more upbeat, I resolved that 2016 would rank as our best year yet and the first of many more to come.

I cooked some scrambled eggs and sausages, pulled out the champagne glasses, opened a bottle of champagne and took the pitcher of fresh orange juice from the fridge. Susan instantly knew what I was up to; we loaded two trays and went up to the roof terrace, where we sat at the redwood table and savored mimosas with our breakfast. We stayed there until it was nearly noon, just quietly basking in each other's attention and enjoying the love we share for one another.

Finally, we got up to walk around our property. The green grass of summer was long gone, replaced by its winter yellow; the verdure of our olive trees contrasted with the grass, as did the garlic patch. I pulled out my iPhone and started taking pictures, deciding that every year I would document the growth of our crops from one year to the next. Checking out the trees, the gardens and the progress on the stone planting beds being erected felt good.

It felt so good, in fact, that we grabbed another bottle of champagne and headed back to our perch, where we could admire our property from a three-hundred-sixty-degree view. I went downstairs and turned on our stereo system. The gentle Tony Bennet, Frank Sinatra and Barbra Streisand music flowed from all the speakers on the terrace; I could control the volume and the music with my iPhone.

Finally putting the past behind us, we focused on the New Year; we started talking over each another about all the outrageous things we wanted to do. We decided that we would go to the jewelry store on the next day and look at the space again; if we had a favorable impression of it, we would place our store there. When we came down from the terrace at three o'clock in the afternoon, I sat in the den to watch some football; once in a while, I would glance at my Christ and feel good.

Close to noon on January 2, we walked into the jewelry store and examined it; when we had visited for the first time, we had been so upset about the market deal having fallen through that we could not evaluate the place fairly. We liked what we saw. The ceiling in the main room was about thirty feet high and made of a plastic laminate that let in a lot of light. All the walls were covered with chunks of pink and gray cantera stone, which would normally be found in an opal mine; indeed, the store looked like a mine and was called The Opal Mine. Rough-cut timber and wood were placed to give the appearance of supporting rock inside a mine. Well lit to showcase the fine jewelry, the display cases resembled mine cars and sat on real tracks; additional wall display cases were made from hanging wheelbarrows. This was not a cheap jewelry store.

The space available for our store was just to the left of the center of the store and totally empty. Next to it was a small room that had once been a bathroom, as indicated by a hole in the floor, which was stuffed with newspaper, and a tiled shower at one end. Our main space was approximately two hundred square feet; the floor was tiled and had been painted red at some point, while the beamed-tile ceiling was nearly sixteen feet high and had a little one-square-foot glass skylight with chipped red paint on it. There were no lights or electrical outlets. We were not enamored of the place but were not against it; one can say that we were neutral, probably because we were eager to start selling our olive oil.

Gregorio, the storeowner, was there and had already visited our farm store; he is a young Mexican man in his early forties and speaks English. He told me he has a store in Puerto Vallarta and had signed a long-term lease for the store in SMA. Susan and I liked him right away; more importantly, we trusted him. His proposal to us was very good, so we accepted it; he would be sending the lease papers later in the day to our e-mail address. We were also informed that there would be an inauguration and cocktail party on January 15. Five days later, everything had been signed and we began an aggressive campaign to renovate the space.

Learning from our Five Chefs event, we decided to use wooden pallets to cover the walls and fit our shelves into. Transito and Juan went into full gear; within two hours, they had brought a load of pallets and were nailing them to the walls of our space. We then called our ironworker, who was also there within the hour, and measured for a door to the closet (the old bathroom) and for shelves to be fitted to the pallets. Our electrician arrived shortly, and we agreed on what was to be done.

Susan had taken grayish and pinkish cantera stone chips from the store; we went to our paint supplier and mixed a gallon of paint for each color, matching the stone as much as possible. By January 14, our store had been totally outfitted. We had brought in one of the cabinets from our country store, which both provided storage and displayed our products. Our crescent-moon-shaped tasting bar was also moved into the store, and a new mesquite counter was made for Zandunga.

All that remained was to bring in our product inventory. Our printer had promised a new batch of labels by five o'clock in the afternoon on the fourteenth, and we headed home with the labels. The olive oils had been bottled and the boxes marked so we could affix the correct label to the oils.

When we came home, however, we were shocked. Our printing house had thought that we wanted labels for the fifty-milliliter bottles, which we planned to use in our gift boxes; we had no labels for two-hundred-fifty-milliliter bottles and no chance that they would be finished until the following week. We decided that we would print our own labels; we had sufficient stock of not only the adhesive labels but also ink cartridges for the printer. And so we went to work; by the middle of the next day, the inventory was placed on the shelf and ready for sale. There was just enough time to go home, change our clothes and make it back to the store.

The Spanish word for street is *calle*, and the word for alley is *callejón*. In SMA, one can get a permit for a *Callejonada,* a parade through a certain street route during which people follow a burro and a band while drinking a lot of mezcal and tequila.

Gregorio had scheduled a callejonada for the grand opening, and the parade ended at the store; it began at around seven o'clock in the morning, and by eight o'clock people started coming into the store. The place was packed; we did not have much time to think, so we just reacted to the crowd. Our little space was full of people holding glasses of wine and generally making merry. Mary Ellen and Jordi showed up in the nick of time and served tapenade hors d'oeuvres throughout the store; I was busily presenting tastings, Susan was cooking more hors d'oeuvres, Rosa was collecting the money and Marisol and Transito were bagging. Time flew by; we were selling for three hours, and during that time our sales nearly exceeded a month's worth at Zandunga.

A lot of our shoppers were English speakers. Susan and I decided that we would run the store daily until we had a good feel for the traffic so we could figure out how much staff support we needed. Transito and Rosa would still handle the Zandunga events.

As the month progressed, many people were asking to visit our farm. We decided to create in-store advertising for farm tours that would require at least four people and provide a lunch for approximately fifteen dollars per person. Once we were organized, we put a table seating six to eight people in the store and began to conduct our tours. Our lunch menu started with whatever vegetables we had available at the farm, and we built it from there; we would also check with the guests to ensure that we were taking personal dietary needs into consideration.

Amid this activity, at times my chest felt as if it was going to explode; however, I stayed calm because I knew that my costochondritis was flaring up. In early January, I had my periodic blood analysis done; it showed one of the markers for inflammation to be through the roof, but it could have been a false reading. A second test for the same marker was normal a week later. Although I had made two visits to Dr. Barrera because of the pains, he had found nothing; finally, he told me it was all in my head. I had said that may be so, but my chest got all these pings and pangs and sometimes it drove me crazy.

Mary Ellen had given me a little pamphlet about a product called olive leaf extract, which I had set aside on top of a coffee table. On a cold January night, having started a roaring fire in the fireplace, I sat down and began reading the book; only about thirty pages long, it discusses the analysis, benefits and other attributes of an extract from olive leaves that has been made for thousand of years. When I was halfway through the book, Susan passed by and I told her that this stuff sounded really great; maybe we should make some so I could take it for my pains. Susan replied, "Why don't you start taking it right away? We have it in the closet; we bought it last year in the States."

I did start taking the extract right away, several drops each morning with juice. Within three days, I was feeling much better, and the pains subsided over the next few weeks until they were gone.

Press Coverage: February 2016

The results of the extract that I personally experienced were so good that I immediately researched the best way to make it; once it was ready, I planned to take it myself. By the end of February, I was feeling great, so I decided to put it in a small bottle with a dropper and give it away at the store. We have customers with a myriad of ailments who come by for their little bottles on a regular basis; many have written or commented on the benefits they have derived. I am now wholesaling it to people from Mexico City and bottling and selling it under their brand; we charge over three hundred dollars per liter.

At the beginning of the month, Transito and I were interviewed by a local online newspaper. The article was written entirely in Spanish; I love the opening paragraph, which translated as follows:

"In a land where all you hear is the wind, you will find Finca Luna Serena, a magical place where you will find more than one thousand three hundred planted olive trees that maintain a Mexican family and an American family united. It is a place where they plant, harvest, prepare, cook, process, season and flavor tons of fine oils; you breathe tranquility and flavor because in the same space the Mexican and American traditions are also united."

The whole Spanish article is available at http://newssanmiguel.com/?p=8599.

The sales performance for the first four weeks exceeded our expectations; we had purposely projected that we would break even. Our hours at the store are from eleven o'clock in the morning until six thirty at night six days a week; we are closed on Tuesdays. Its traffic is much heavier on weekends and holidays; the traffic during each day is predictable: light between eleven in the morning and one in the afternoon, progressively heavier between one and five in the afternoon, and light between five and six thirty in the evening. While at the store, I made sure that my time was productive during the slow period; I always brought my briefcase, laptop and iPad, and the jewelry store was equipped with Wi-Fi, so I was fully connected. My work varied between reading about olives and olive oil, developing plans and forecasts and working on our various webpages. I cleaned up and updated our homepage, and we started using the address www.fincalunarena.com in all of our promotional materials, including labels; with Marisol's aid, our website was written in both English and Spanish, and it read very nicely.

When I started focusing on promotional activities, I found that Facebook was a useful conduit, so I began studying how to develop effective pages with really good, crisp copy, use boosting as an advertising vehicle and gear advertising to specific audiences and demographics; I was in my element. I also learned to develop a public page for the store, keeping my private page private. It was not easy; Facebook is a tool with many facets that one has to navigate in order to get things done within its framework.

One of my earliest lessons was writing an effective Facebook post. For my first post, I announced the grand opening of our store and then ran it as a two-week campaign. When a campaign is boosted, the advertisement randomly appears on the Facebook newsfeed whenever a person is logged in; the person can then either ignore the ad or click on it and get more information. Upon clicking, the person may choose to react to the ad by either liking or disliking it. Once my post went live, I checked several hours later and found that I was getting more dislikes than likes. I had no idea why I was getting such a reaction, so I spent time reviewing the ad; the only thing I thought could be wrong was that the ad was in English. As soon as I converted the ad's copy into Spanish, the response was extremely positive with no dislikes.

Another major side benefit of Facebook to me was that I could reconnect with my former business colleagues throughout the world, including all my New York comrades I had left behind in June 2014. I was beginning to feel alive again; one might say my oscillating life was on an upswing. As I slowly became more proficient on Facebook, through my posts I started making new friends as well as renewing old acquaintances; the feeling that I got while sending messages and even exchanging pictures with them was very surprising.

On my private Facebook page, I have over two hundred friends. I do not collect friends; these are all people with whom I have crossed paths in a meaningful way. Many of them like to regularly post things they find on the Internet that interest them and that they feel may be of interest to others. Some constantly express their political views. As for me, I prefer to post about things happening in my life that I want to share with my friends; most of my posts are pictures or videos, as was the case when the monarch butterflies visited. A friend even asked to use this video in one of her children's grammar school classes, as they were studying the butterflies' migration. I especially love to post what I am seeing at the moment, whether a sunset, a bird captured in flight, horses, sheep, chickens or the burro.

Since I had not previously mentioned the burro, here is the story. Several years earlier, Transito had asked us to buy a burro he could use to pull a plow. While our soil is very fertile, it also has a lot of stones; I believe our soil is volcanic, and it feels like clay when it is wet and hardens when it is dry. Using hand tools to prepare this soil for planting can indeed be a daunting task, but I had not wanted a burro, so I had ignored the request until we had started a very large vegetable garden to plant corn or garlic.

Finally, I had decided to buy Transito a heavy-duty rototiller, which is a heavy machine with a thirteen-horsepower gasoline engine. Although the machine works just fine, it would not have lasted two years but for Transito's mechanical skills. The rocks in our soil get stuck on the tines, and the machine has to be shut off before the rocks can be removed; starting, stopping and restarting the rototiller can sometimes get the better of Transito's patience. As Transito had prepared the rototiller in January for use in February, he had kept bellyaching that we needed a burro.

While I like things to be in harmony on our farm, and the rototiller had clearly caused consternation, I had thought we could live with it. Then suddenly I had seen the light and told Transito that he could have a burro. So, what had changed my mind? I had recognized the advantage to our business, of course; with our tours increasing and people making plans to rent our cottage, I had concluded that a burro could offer many more benefits than just contributing to our fertilizer factory.

On February 1, Transito came home with the burro, a cute little guy less than three years old. He had been kept in a pen for his entire life, so he is tame and friendly. The camera on my phone started clicking away; I decided to hold a "name that burro" contest with my friends on Facebook, so I posted it on my Facebook page. We received quite a few entries, and we finally selected Valentino, after Rudolph Valentino.

I have yet to see Valentino pull a plow, but Transito says he needs to make some parts for the plow and then train Valentino. In the meantime, Transito has put the horse saddles on him and visiting children have been riding him.

Valentino is quite a character and fun to watch. We had purchased a big blue ball with a handle for the horses to counter corral boredom; they have never used it, but Valentino plays soccer with it, flipping, kicking and running after the ball. We have a very large riding arena about fifty feet wide and one hundred feet long that has a deep sand cover; I have seen Valentino run a lap around it at full gallop, then pace for a few minutes and start again as if training for a race. Lately, Susan has been saying he is lonely, so there may be a Valentina in his future.

During the last harvest season, our fruit trees had served as a source for vinegars, juices and jellies, and I was concerned that the jellies in particular would not sell. We had managed to accumulate ten different kinds of jelly, including grape jelly made from grapes gifted to us by the local winery. In mid-February, we decided to give a tasting of our jelly to a prospective customer. To my surprise, they became very popular thereafter.

By the third week in February, Susan and I had gotten a good feel for the traffic at the store, so we determined that we needed someone responsible who understood the business. Evaluating our staff, we debated whether Rosa should shift from the farm to the store, but after a while we came to the conclusion that Rosa was key to our overall production; we finally decided to close the stand operated by Irma and bring her to the new store.

While the stand was generating a slight profit, the sales at our store in one week would be greater than the monthly sales at the stand; transferring Irma would allow us to more efficiently utilize her substantial experience in selling our products. Rosa would join her during weekends, since we knew the store would require two staff members during those busy days. Although Susan and I helped Irma for the first few weeks, by mid-March we no longer had to be present; we then developed a schedule allowing each of us to work only three days at the store in town.

Gregorio, our landlord and the owner of the jewelry store, lives in Puerto Vallarta, where his original Opal Mine store is located. From the day we signed the lease, we felt close to him and his family, and our friendship intensified over time. By the end of February, our relationship had become so tightly knit that they were like family. Gregorio's entire family came to visit, and we bonded even further.

Olive-oil Tastings: March 2016

We kept the publicity machine running, and at the beginning of March we had another major online article featuring us. This one was in English but could be instantly translated in to Spanish. I love the headline, "Pressing Matters," followed by a big wonderful picture of Susan in our store with our olive oils and tasting counter in the background. ~~Here is a link to the article:~~

~~http://loccal.org/articles/2016/march/fincaa.php~~

During the first three months of operating our store inside The Opal Mine, we had honed our skills in presenting our olive oil. It was no longer possible to have people taste our oil sprinkled all over small pieces of bread; instead, we chose to conduct the tastings utilizing one-ounce plastic cups.

Using the early lessons from my reading, I began to educate myself on how to taste olive oil, particularly natural oils. Olive oil is usually tasted in a small blue cup in order to mask the true color of the oil; since an oil's color has nothing to do with its quality or taste, the color is concealed so people are not influenced by it. Once the oil is poured into the blue cup, one holds the cup in the palms of one's hands and warms it; after a few minutes, one sips some of the oil, rolling it around in one's mouth before swallowing as one takes a deep breath. This is the way it is done professionally in order to experience the true taste of the olive oil.

We could not locate the little cups, so we developed our own similar method. After pouring the olive oil into small plastic cups, I taught our customers how to taste olive oil. My procedure was simple: one takes some oil into one's mouth without swallowing, then rolls it around one's palate with one's tongue for twenty to thirty seconds; finally, one swallows and inhales through one's mouth. One thus experiences the different flavors in the olive oil. I would then describe the tastes that I had detected in the oil; often, I would taste the oil along with the customer, and we would compare the various flavors we were sensing. During this process, I came to realize that people do not taste the same things; in my case, olive oil always has a strong almond or other nutty flavor.

Over the first three months of 2016, I had gained a lot of experience in conducting the tastings, even becoming familiar with people's reactions to our flavored oils. We had infused olive oil with lemon, oregano, basil, rosemary, garlic and black truffle; in addition, Susan had brought from New York last Thanksgiving a bottle of smoked olive oil. I had read that this oil was gaining popularity in some parts of the United States, so I decided to create our own smoked olive oil. Utilizing apple wood in our Kamado grill, I experimented with smoking olive oil until I achieved success. In the process, I added sliced chile de arból, a fairly hot chili pepper that Transito grows on our property; the resulting oil is smoky and flavorful, and although it is not spicy, it finishes with a slight tingle from the chili pepper.

I felt extremely proud of the quality of our olive oil until I had a discussion with one of our consultants. Since he was knowledgeable about olive oil, I decided to give him a tasting similar to the ones that I was giving at the store. When he confirmed that he too was getting the nutty almond flavor, I was truly excited. Then he said, "But Victor, don't you know that when olive oil has a residual taste of almonds it is a bad oil?" Upon hearing this, I was devastated and embarrassed; I had presented so many tastings and misled people into thinking that we had great olive oil.

Demoralized and not knowing where to turn for comfort, I walked around in a sad state of confusion, which became anger at myself and finally total depression that lasted for the next couple of days. Then, during one of my nightly readings, I decided to Google what the taste of olive oil should be; I found what I was looking for fairly quickly. The following is a list that I obtained from one of the major oil manufacturers of the various tastes that one should look for in olive oil. Many of our customers had these sensations.

Positive attributes of extra virgin olive oil
Almond: flavor typical of fresh or dried almond. This is retro-nasal aroma, normally associated with sweet oils.
Apple: apple-flavored oil.
Artichoke: oil that tastes like tender part of an artichoke.
Bitter: a characteristic flavor of oil made from green olives.

The bitterness should not be too strong; otherwise it would be considered a defect.

Floral: delicate flavor of white or yellow flowers.

Fruity: flavor of the oil that recalls the aroma and flavor of fresh, perfectly ripe fruit. Upon tasting the oil, you can begin to make the distinction between intense and delicate fruitiness. This former is direct, where as the latter is finer and less biting, both directly in the mouth and with regards to the retro-nasal aromas.

Green herbs: flavor reminiscent of the aroma of freshly cut grass.

Olio verde (Green Oil): the classic characteristic of Tuscan oils; great, fruit aromas, and bright green color.

Ripeness: characteristic flavor of ripe olives often found in bright yellow-colored oils with round, sweet flavors.

Roundness: oil that is full and well rounded.

Sweet: oil is considered sweet if it has a light flavor and delicate aroma.

Spicy: biting sensation that is characteristic of olive grown at the beginning of the countryside, and that are primarily still green. It is a pleasing aspect typical of oils from Tuscany, Puglia, and Sicily. In order for spiciness to be considered a positive aspect of the oil, the sensation should be fleeting.

Spices/Vegetables/Apple: flavor associated with vegetal or spiced aromas.

There is also a list of the negative attributes of olive oil.

I finally decided that I would let the consultant continue to believe what he told me to be true. There is no sense in arguing with people, particularly when one knows one is right; I am still proud of our product.

In March, I was extremely proud of what we were doing and full of a wonderful feeling about the coming spring; I was taking pictures of our trees in bloom, and life was just marvelous. On March 9, I was sitting in my recliner, watching the CBS evening news, when awe and panic struck at the same time. From my recliner, I have a perfect view of the backyard and the distant mountains; it was the twilight of a dark and gloomy day. During a commercial break, I was staring out aimlessly and then noticed that it was possibly snowing outside. After grabbing my iPhone and walking outside, I was in disbelief that it was indeed snowing; I made a one-minute video and narrated what was happening as I filmed. Once I got past the wonder of it, I began to worry about the potential impact that the snow would have on our blooming fruit and olive trees. Since there was nothing much I could do about the forces of nature, I decided to wait until the next day to survey the damage.

There was a little snow accumulation in some areas; many of my friends were posting pictures on Facebook of their snow experiences. Quite a large portion of Mexico received the dusting of snow, though I call it a dusting based on New York standards; as far as the Mexicans were concerned, this was a blizzard! Over the next couple of days, I kept checking our blooms and again we were blessed—we suffered no damage.

Neither rain nor sleet nor snow could keep us from developing our tourism destination. We continued planting olive trees, but we focused on a Greek variety known as "Koroneiki"; we planted one hundred of these trees and dreamt of someday harvesting the olives and making oil from them.

I should mention at this point that because of the exposure gained in our store, people began to visit our farm for tours and lunches, as well as to purchase goods at our farm store. Our farm sales for the first three months of the year were nearly fifteen percent of the total sales achieved by the store in SMA.

During a trip to one of the nearby cities, I stopped at a major retailer to check out a redwood bar set with three stools, thinking that it would look good on the roof terrace. I spent a lot of time studying it; while I was doing so, a young man in his mid-thirties opened up a discussion about the redwood set. Over the course of the conversation, it became evident to me that he worked at the store. As we were saying goodbye, he asked me what it was like to live in SMA; surprised by the question, I gently teased, "Are you in the habit of thinking that because people look like Americans, they consequently live in the town of San Miguel de Allende?" He apologized, and I laughed, letting him know that his query did not really bother me.

During the ensuing conversation, he told me he was interested in SMA and would like to build a house there; I asked him where, and when he told me the development he was looking at, I told him I thought it was pricey. He smiled and said he was partial to the place because he wanted to live out in the countryside, to which I replied that if he wished to reside in the country in SMA, he should consider renting a house there and seeing what it is like; when he agreed, I offered him our cottage for rent.

He asked whether I would offer him a good deal, and of course I said yes; I then told him he could find information about the cottage on our website, and he said he would go to his office to check it out. As he was starting to leave, I inquired what his name was, and he said Victor Gutierrez; surprised, I laughed and said, "You've got to be kidding." When he indignantly demanded to know why, I handed him my card and he cracked up when he looked at it. When he gave me his card, I saw that he was the manager of the store.

We went on our way and continued shopping. Not fifteen minutes had passed when he found us walking among the aisles and asked whether we would rent the house to him. I said of course we would, and two days later he and his family rented the house for ten days.

Our sales were growing substantially every month; in fact, our plan was coming together in all respects but one—I still had not finished the book about the first fifteen years we had owned our property in Mexico. Slowly, I began to re-edit the book; each time was more depressing because I would continue to find errors and rewrite sections. It was sheer agony.

<u>Rock Star??</u><s>Expanding Horizons</s>: **April 2016**

By the beginning of April, the store was running smoothly under the charge of Susan and Irma; I only needed to go once in a while to give Susan a respite. The store also served as a promotion for our farm store and our tours.

The response to our tours was very favorable; our chickens were laying a lot of eggs, so we decided to start offering a tour with a breakfast. Using the little portable stoves that we had purchased at the Korean store, I made individual omelets with all the ingredients one would find in a restaurant. In addition to eggs and omelets, María cooked *chileaquiles*. Fresh orange juice and home-roasted coffee rounded out a full breakfast for the tour that lasted approximately three hours.

Even though the store and the farm were performing better than planned, we kept promoting and scheduling events. Earlier in the year, we had purchased a stand at an event called Wine and Paella; held at the same venue where the Five Chefs event took place in October, it was projected to have an attendance of more than one thousand people.

Attached to the large events hall, a tented area seating three hundred people had been added; all the attendees entered through this area. We had a choice location at the third stand from the entrance, and the turnout proved to be as predicted; it was an excellent event for us. The promoters at the Five Chefs event once again welcomed us with open arms as if we were family; they also ensured that every dignitary visited our stand and tasted our olive oil. Our sales were terrific, and this time we did recoup the cost of our stand. Moreover, we made several important connections that would drive our future sales; one customer at this event would later come to our store, become a good friend and purchase our olive leaf extract in bulk to be sold in Mexico City, which would lead to our development of other medicinal olive products.

As the event was concluding, a young couple from the nearby city of León approached us. Several days earlier, our organic consultant, who resides in León, had telephoned and asked us whether we would like to be involved in a project there; it had been a somewhat convoluted discussion, but I had quickly gathered that the consultant wanted the principals of the project to meet us. The only thing that had been clear from the conversation was that we had been chosen to be the preferred processor of the fruits from the trees being planted in a housing development.

The date he had had in mind for a meeting had been the same as that of the event, and I had told him we could not do it; unbeknownst to me, he had then informed the owners of the development, and they had decided to partake in the festivities and speak with us there. And so as we were wrapping up the remaining inventory from the event, this young couple walked up to our stand and introduced themselves.

They were a young married couple named Adriana and Nestor. When I sat down with them while she drank her scotch and he his beer, they gave me a brief explanation of the project, but I was still not one hundred percent clear about it; we all agreed that they would meet us at our farm on the next day to discuss it in complete detail. However, on the following day they sent a message that they were not feeling well and would have to postpone the appointment.

Things were moving right along at the farm. Our zucchini plants began to yield quite a large amount; as we were having lunches scheduled at the farm, we taught María and Rosa how to make zucchini pancakes and zucchini cake.

Our typical lunch menu for tours was
>An olive-oil tasting
>Olives and tapenade at the center of the table
>A green salad with tomatoes and onions from our garden
>Stewed tomatoes and chayote
>Chicken chipotle
>Mexican red rice
>Zucchini pancakes
>Zucchini cake with a scoop of our olive-oil ice cream

Our fee per person was four hundred pesos, or approximately twenty-five dollars. Including a forty-five-minute discussion tour, the total time was approximately three hours. Invariably, our guests also purchased a good deal of our products. We limited our tours to one group at a time; since groups made the reservations, everybody knew each other.

As I quickly skim through the pictures for this timeframe, I can clearly see that our little farm was responding to the organic fertilizer that was being applied. For instance, our Swiss chard had leaves almost two feet long, the garlic that we harvested during this month was nearly three to four inches in diameter and the greenhouse was beginning to look like a jungle. Consequently, when one reviews our menu one will observe that about the only things we were not producing were the chicken and the rice. We knew that our generous servings did not result in much additional profit to us, but we wanted people to come back so we as well as our staff could gain experience.

Adriana and Nestor came to our farm during the week following the event; finally, we got a clear picture of their project. They own approximately six acres inside a prestigious golfing community in León, and they had planned an ecologically friendly walled neighborhood that was to contain ten individual lots separated by cleverly designed borders of fruit-bearing trees and plants that were to be mostly olive trees. At this point, they had invested a good deal of money in architectural design, laying out two streets and subdividing property; in addition, they had already installed the necessary utility connections for the homes to be erected on the lots. We had been selected to process the olives and make olive oil.

Adriana and Nestor were selling the lots and planning an event to take place in León on April 27. According to Adriana, approximately twenty-five prominent couples from León were invited to attend a cocktail party and dinner reception; during the event, a presentation (sales pitch) would be made to the couples. We would be announced as the processor of the olives and be giving olive-oil tastings to the guests.

Susan and I left home on April 26 at around midday; driving to León was a new experience for us, as we had never been to the city of León. Only the road leading into it was familiar to us because we had flown in and out of the León airport, situated approximately fifteen miles from the center of the city, many times. As we approached the city, the traffic became more congested. We had arranged to meet Adriana and Nestor at the specific address where the building for the event was located; based on the various GPS devices that we had brought along, we came to the appointed address. However, we were in front of a shoe store, and we were supposed to be facing a seven-story building that Adriana had described; we called her, and she asked us to send her our location. I was not sure how to do that, but she gave me instructions on using an app called WhatsApp; I thought it was cool that I could tell her where I was with my phone. In a few minutes, she and Nestor arrived, and they guided us to the locale.

We drove into the downstairs parking lot of a very modern building. On the way to this location, we were making mental notes of all the shopping opportunities available within minutes of our destination; Wal-Mart, Costco and Home Depot were prominent, as well as many others.

We then went upstairs to the top floor of the building, a very modern area consisting of a large room approximately forty feet long and wide that contained a small bar in one corner and a foyer-like seating area, as well as a huge terrace partly under the roof; this was where the event would take place. The guests' arrival was scheduled for the next day at approximately eight o'clock at night, followed by a cocktail reception, after which Adriana, the architects, the organic consultant and we would make presentations. An international chef had been hired to provide cocktail tapas and would also be preparing a dinner after the presentations; the food would be grilled over an olivewood fire, and we had brought the olivewood. As Adriana talked us through the planned event, we used our imaginations because nothing was set up; that phase would commence on the subsequent day.

After conferring for about two hours, Susan and I left and checked into the Crown Plaza Hotel. A few hours later, we were picked up by our hosts and driven to a nearby Argentine beef restaurant; there we had further discussions with them and agreed that we would meet on the next day at ten o'clock in the morning to prepare.

On the following day, Susan and I had breakfast at the hotel, then drove to the building where we would be making the presentation. We arrived before anyone else, so we started preparing our presentation; fortunately, I had my laptop with me, which contained a lot of material about olive oil. I was able to put a decent presentation together over the course of the next several hours; from my computer, I utilized information on the history of olive oil as well as some pictures I had taken of our farm and of our store.

As the day progressed, we saw the event venue taking shape. The main room had been set up by five o'clock in the afternoon. All the tables were arranged in a U-shape, accommodating approximately thirty people facing the presentation area, and three big-screen televisions for the guests to view were installed in front of the tables. Lots of flowers adorned the reception area, and the bar was being prepared and stocked.

Adriana was nervously trying to put her presentation together when Susan and I left to change clothes for the event. I decided to keep it simple by wearing black slacks and a black shirt; Susan wore cream-colored slacks with a salmon-colored top.

We were back at the event venue by six thirty that evening. Some preparations still remained to be done, but all seemed under control. Just before eight o'clock, Adriana and Nestor arrived. Adriana told me that this would be her very first presentation in front of a group; she was clearly nervous. I assured her that everything would turn out fine; she just had to be herself.

In discussions with Adriana, it was agreed that the event presentations would begin with our organic consultant, followed by our presentation and tasting. I had prepared a slide presentation about fifteen minutes long about the history of olive oil and a short history of Finca Luna Serena. Then I would conduct an olive-oil tasting. With so many people and a limited amount of time, I had decided to present two natural olive oils and two flavored olive oils; therefore, before anyone had arrived we had set four small empty brandy glasses in front of each guest's seat.

Night had already fallen, and the building we were in was located at a point high above the city. One whole wall of the room was glass, and the lights of the city shimmered below; with this background, the room was resplendent. Its soft lighting accented the deep-blue tablecloths and the small brandy glasses in front of each seat. The widescreen televisions gave a thoroughly professional look to the room. At the rear, the bar had been arranged with cheeses, crackers, breads and an array of all our products inclusive of oils, olives and jellies.

One characteristic of Mexico is that very few things start on time; when no one had arrived at eight fifteen, we all had slightly nervous looks on our faces, but the worry was soon over as people began coming. Everything seemed hazy to me; I was about to make a professional presentation to a crowd that we had never met, and I did not know what the reception would be like. While the cocktail party was in progress, Susan and I filled the small glasses with the four olive oils that we had selected; I was familiar with the oils' tastes and could thoroughly describe them.

By nine thirty, people began to be seated around the tables. In the last few minutes, we had slightly altered the agenda; since the glasses would be in the way, it had been decided that I would be the first presenter. Adriana started with a very short summary of the project, then launched into my introduction. In my mind, I seemed to float into the center of the presentation area. After leading with the history of olive oil as explained in the slides, I briefly discussed our farm; before long, I went into the tasting phase. As I commenced this segment, I knew that the audience was already on my side; I had seen them nod, smile and even help me with some of the words I had struggled with in Spanish. When I presented the olive oils and explained how to taste them, people became more animated and loved the tasting. Soon my presentation was over, and as I thanked them for their attention the audience gave me a standing ovation; at that moment, I felt like a rock star and my adrenaline was running incredibly high. Afterward, Adriana hugged me and said, "You have given me much inspiration." She then proceeded to conduct the rest of the event with slideshows, architects and descriptions of their concept for their small community.

After the presentations, people proceeded to the outdoor terrace for a night of eating, drinking, dancing and even a flamenco show—all under the stars in a cloudless sky. Susan and I departed at around midnight, and I believe that we were the first to leave.

The Idles of May 2016

Having finished an incredibly hectic four months focused on growing our business, we were totally unprepared for the low that was to come during the month of May. As mentioned earlier, Susan and I were learning about the retail aspects of our business; one of the lessons that we would have is that May is a commercially dead month it finished so weakly that our sales for the last week in April proved to be greater than the sales for the entire month of May. We also observed that this was not just affecting us; for quite a few days, the jewelry store as well as ours had absolutely no customers walking in. Apparently, very few tourists come to SMA during the month of May, and many of the expatriates living in SMA leave for vacation at the same time. Not only is the town empty, but also the heat at times can be in excess of ninety degrees each day; these temperatures continue until the summer rains break the pattern.

However, we did manage to book one lunch tour during the month, which gave us the opportunity to try out another menu item. I had read that it is a tradition in some olive oil–producing countries for the producer to taste his or her fresh olive oil on bread that has been toasted over an olivewood fire, and we added this course to our menu immediately following the olive-oil tasting. We set up one of our mesquite tasting counters under a canopy, Transito toasted French bread on an olivewood fire and on the table we placed a bowl of our tomatoes that had been cut in half, as well as a dish of our freshly harvested garlic also sliced in large pieces. After finishing the olive-oil tasting in the store, we led the group to the counter; as Transito toasted the bread, our guests were instructed to rub the warm bread with garlic and then tomato, topping it off with the olive oil of their choice. The reaction was very positive; one of them said, "With a bottle of wine, we do not need to have lunch," which was exactly the response that we were looking for. While we did provide lunch that day, Susan and I were already developing a change in our tour offerings and pricing; it took us from the middle of May through part of June to finalize our card handouts and Facebook posts. Here are the new tour offerings that would begin on July 1:

Tour One: The Olive Experience
> Starts at 11:00 a.m. Monday through Saturday. Minimum four people. Approximately 90 minutes.
> 250 pesos per person

> Enjoy a leisurely walk for approximately 45 minutes learning about the growing of olives in a sustainable organic environment supplemented with light agriculture and farm animals.

> After our walk, we will return to the farm store for a description of the making of olive oil and the curing of olives. This includes a tasting of the Finca Luna Serena oils, olives and tapenade.

Finally, we will enjoy traditional bruschetta. It is a tradition that after the pressing of olives, the producer immediately tastes his oil quality by toasting bread on an olivewood fire, then rubbing the bread with either garlic, tomato or salt and smothering it with the fresh olive oil. Gluten-free bread is provided with prior arrangement.

Tour Two: A Country Lunch
Starts at 1:00 p.m. Monday through Saturday. Minimum four people. Approximately 3 hours. 400 pesos per person

This tour includes all of the aspects of Tour One plus a simple and delicious country lunch with a glass of wine or beer. Lunch could be a quiche, a frittata or a potpie with a salad and dessert. We always try to utilize fresh fruits, vegetables and eggs from the farm whenever possible and are happy to adjust to accommodate particular needs and preferences. And, of course, you are welcome to bring additional wine or beer if you like.

Tour Three: Bring Your Friends and Family to a Picnic!
Starts at 2:00 p.m. or earlier, depending on season. Minimum six people. Approximately 5 hours. 900 pesos per person

Enjoy a relaxed afternoon in the San Miguel de Allende countryside. We start with the walking tour, educational talks, tastings and bruschetta of Tour One. Then you will be treated to a gourmet four-course buffet meal under the trees (weather permitting). We will work with you to create the perfect menu for your group using as many foods from the farm as possible. If this is a special occasion like a birthday or other celebration, we are happy to take the extra steps to make it wonderful!

Transportation available from Luciérnaga (Liverpool) if needed.

Tours conducted in English or Spanish.

For reservations, write to info@fincalunaserena.com.

Irrespective of the local sales activity, production at the farm had to be maintained; watering and fertilizing the trees in preparation for the summer rains were crucial. Supply and inventory levels were being recorded, and planning for the heavy production season to begin in late June was already taking place.

I do not want to paint a rosy picture; it really was a lousy month that ended up even worse. On the evening of May 31, we had a severe hailstorm; I was very concerned not only for the fruit trees but also for all the olive trees were already at the fruiting stage. Again, I waited until morning to check the damage; fortunately, it was not serious. Some of the fruits were marred and very few were knocked off the trees.

I was glad to see the month pass, and the only good thing that came of this experience was that we knew from then on we would be taking vacations during May.

A Two-year Review: June 2016

We began the month of June full of activity and great expectations. First, we signed a contract for an outdoor sign that was to be located one mile from the entrance to the town of SMA; the road on which it was placed is considered the main thoroughfare if one is coming from Mexico City, Querétaro and points south. Susan and I decided to keep the signage simple; set in a black background was our olive-moon logo with "Finca Luna Serena" below and to the left along with bright yellow copy to the right that is translated as follows:

> Extra-virgin Olive Oil,
> Vinegar and Olives
> Taste the Difference
> Made in
> San Miguel de Allende
> Hernandez Macias #99

We had high hopes that the sign would help put our name out to the general public. Since it was a six-month contract, if we did not feel it worked properly we could terminate it after six months.

Supporting our promotional activities, we signed up for three events during the month of June. The first was an industry event for suppliers of hotels and restaurants that was held at the new San Miguel Convention Center in La Casona; it was a two-day event that was not expected to yield a great deal of immediate sales. As we expected, we made a lot of contacts from hotel owners to restaurateurs, all of who were interested in utilizing our olive oil for their businesses; subsequent visits to them resulted in a steady stream of wholesale business.

The second event, called Mezcal y Borrego, was a one-day afternoon affair that was very entertaining; it was primarily a competition among chefs and restaurants to determine which of them cooked the best lamb. As the name implies, there was also mezcal; one could get as much as one wanted to drink and all the lamb one wished to eat. Again, we made many contacts with new chefs and the general public in attendance.

The final event was a repeat performance of the previous year's Sabores San Miguel, except this year we were better prepared. We limited the number of products we were presenting so the presentation was faster and easier; in addition, we had a larger selection of small dishes to sell. Our sales on the first day, which was Friday night, exceeded the sales achieved during the entire three-day period of the prior year. Of course, Jordi and Mary Ellen came by and lent a hand on Saturday afternoon, doing the same things they did last year. When the event ended, our sales were more than double those from our first year; obviously, it was a complete success.

Looking back over the last twenty-four months, there were many ups and downs; we faced many obstacles but tried to convert each of them into a positive, and we were successful most of the time. We have yet to find our perfect dark glass bottle, but we are satisfied with what we have and explain to people that our olive oil does not last long enough in the bottle for it to go bad, which is indeed the case at our home. Furthermore, we have eaten oil that we stored for ourselves from the first few days of making oil; even though it is two years old, it still tastes like it did on the day we made it.

We have not been able to establish an online ordering and delivering capability. The major obstacle here is the lack of affordable delivery costs within Mexico.

We do not own an independent stand-alone store in SMA; however, the current solution of having a store within another store has been very satisfactory and cost efficient.

So, how well did we perform our original objectives overall?

To apply our investments, learning and experience to create an income-generating enterprise, which can sustain current Mexican operations indefinitely by:

> *• Progressively building to achieve an annual net income level by the beginning 2018 that would pay all expenses in Mexico*
>
> Assessment June 30, 2016
> We are clearly on our way to our achieving our goal. Our expenses as projected increased

substantially, but the revenue generated covers the increase as well as part of our going-in cost; therefore, we have no reason to doubt that by the beginning of 2018, Finca Luna Serena will be self-sufficient.

• *Expanding our experiences and lifestyles*

Assessment June 30, 2016
We certainly believe that we have improved our experiences and lifestyles, as well as continue to do so. Producing and processing olives has been quite a challenge; we have had both laughs and tears, but we have enjoyed every minute. Some of our experiences have been detailed in this book, as have some of the lifestyle changes.

If one were to stand out as the biggest change, I would probably say that we have an incredibly memorable experience that happens to be repeated many times over. It is also representative of the kind of lifestyle that Susan and I have planned.

This experience is just the two of us in what we call our Park, located in the middle of our olive grove more than four hundred feet from the house; it usually occurs around sunset, and believe it or not we sit and enjoy the park-like setting of our grove, looking at tall palm trees, hedges and eucalyptus trees. Next to us is a bottle of champagne or tequila, as well as our seven dogs, and not too far away are our movable chicken coops that allow our chickens to range freely and produce what many consider the best organic eggs in town.

• *Expanding and improving the lives of our staff*

Assessment June 30, 2016
Our staff has grown from three to seven people from the same family; to us, they are our family as well. They now are responsible for all the production and serve as the main sales representatives at our store in town. Their lives are improved as a result of the salaries that we pay them, which are considered by many to be higher than the norm, a fact confirmed by direct discussions about this with Transito; they are also provided with many amenities, and we believe their diet is better than that of their compatriots, as they are free to partake in everything that is developed and made on our farm. The entire family has transitioned from manual laborers to artisans in the olive oil–making industry. Many who have spoken with Transito tell us about the pride that he shows when talking about the olive oil that he and his family are making with their own hands.

• *Dramatically improving our health and well-being*

Assessment June 30, 2016

Susan's health is fantastic—no pain, ailments or doctor's appointments. Nothing much needed to be improved on hers two years ago. Mine, on the other hand, has become substantially better over the past two years; I no longer suffer from the common maladies of my previous life before retirement. We did discover a pinched nerve that is causing some problems, but this too is being controlled.

- *Have fun*

Assessment June 30, 2016
We are having fun as we work toward the same goals, which is something we had never done before in our relationship; in the process, we have learned to share responsibilities and tasks and to complement each other. In addition, we go out to dinner two or three times per month and watch movies at least four times per week. Finally, we have mastered living together while giving one another the necessary space.

The approach we would take to achieved the objective was to be

- *Build a rental business from Mexican properties*

Assessment June 30, 2016
We are progressing toward building an income from the rental of properties. This part of our

business did not commence until January 2016; since then, the property has been rented for five different periods, and we are acquiring a reputation for attracting families with children who want to enjoy a tranquil place with the freedom to run around safely. ~~When we developed a Facebook page for the cottage, we received 250 likes in two weeks. Here is the link:~~

~~https://www.facebook.com/Casa-Luna-Serena-276904446000703/~~

• *Develop a line of farm products to take to market*

Assessment June 30, 2016
Clearly, we have been extremely successful in achieving this particular task in our business plan. We have a complete line of olive products, which we continue to expand. In addition, many people purchase our jellies and marmalades, and we sell lots of eggs and even our lambs. However, we have not yet fully explored our organic vegetable production; more training is needed in this regard.

Our market is expanding insofar as we have parties that want to sell our products in at least three other cities as of this writing. Those discussions are currently underway, and I believe they will be fruitful. We are currently wholesaling to 6 restaurants, and there are many more interested.

We are also bringing the market to us by conducting tours and engaging people in our country store.

Driving this entire process is our exposure through events at our store in town. ~~Here is our Facebook page for our store:~~

~~https://www.facebook.com/Fincalunaserena/~~

• *Record experience for potential publishing*

Assessment June 30, 2016
Comparing our performance to our business plan, we find that we are underachieving in only this area. I started spending more time in the office trying to finalize my first book, and the project took over twenty-four months to complete. It was like going back to school all over again; I quickly found out that writing a book is not an easy task. The editing process was painstaking, and I needed Susan's help to finish; however, the more daunting task has proved to be marketing the book. Promoting and selling a book is a business onto itself that I am still learning at the moment.

The struggles with the first book lead to and incredible learning experience and writing has become a new passion.

Here is our Facebook page link for my first book, *The Light of The Serene Moon*:

https://www.amazon.com/Light-Serene-Moon-Retirement-Guanajuato-ebook/dp/B01M9C7LG0/ref=sr_1_3?dchild=1&keywords=the+light+of+the+serene+moon&qid=1610136306&sr=8-3https://www.facebook.com/The-Light-of-the-Serene-Moon-2092359057656154/

Epilogue: November 2016

As we chart the course we have taken over the last two years, it is clear that achievement of the basic plan will be enduring and will have long-lasting effects not only for us but for many other people as well. We are secure in our accomplishments and the direction we have set for ourselves. Many tasks, pitfalls and successes still lay ahead, but we will face or accept them with the same level of intensity as in the previous two years.

Following our plan has been hard work; at times, it has been scary. But most of all, we have had FUN.

I have made a journey from Madison Avenue to the olive grove, accompanied by the best partner I have ever had.

Made in United States
Troutdale, OR
08/06/2023

11841993R00120